The
Miracle
of Levi

A STORY *of* BROKENNESS,
HEALING, MIRACLES, *and*
the POWER *of* PRAYER

CASSIE HYDER LITTLEJOHN

HIGH BRIDGE
BOOKS & MEDIA

The Miracle of Levi
by Cassie Hyder Littlejohn

Copyright © 2025 Cassie Hyder Littlejohn

All rights reserved.

Printed in the United States of America
ISBN: 978-1-962802-25-3

Scripture quotations marked NIV are from THE HOLY BIBLE, NEW INTERNATIONAL VERSION®, NIV® Copyright © 1973, 1978, 1984, 2011 by Biblica, Inc.® Used by permission. All rights reserved worldwide.

Scripture quotations marked NKJV are taken from the New King James Version®. Copyright © 1982 by Thomas Nelson. Used by permission. All rights reserved.

Scripture quotations marked TPT are from The Passion Translation®. Copyright © 2017, 2018, 2020 by Passion & Fire Ministries, Inc. Used by permission. All rights reserved. ThePassionTranslation.com.

Scripture quotations marked ESV are taken from The ESV® Bible (The Holy Bible, English Standard Version®). ESV® Text Edition: 2016. Copyright © 2001 by Crossway, a publishing ministry of Good News Publishers. The ESV® text has been reproduced in cooperation with and by permission of Good News Publishers. Unauthorized reproduction of this publication is prohibited. All rights reserved.

Scripture quotations marked NLT are taken from the *Holy Bible*, New Living Translation, copyright © 1996, 2004, 2015 by Tyndale House Foundation. Used by permission of Tyndale House Publishers, Inc., Carol Stream, Illinois 60188. All rights reserved.

Scripture quotations marked AMP are taken from the Amplified® Bible (AMP), Copyright © 2015 by The Lockman Foundation. Used by permission. lockman.org.

High Bridge Books titles may be purchased in bulk for educational, business, fundraising, or sales promotional use. For information, please contact High Bridge Books via www.HighBridgeBooks.com/contact.

Published in Houston, Texas, by High Bridge Books.

Dedication

I **DEDICATE THIS BOOK TO MY PRECIOUS FAMILY. WE ALL** walked through this trial together and I could not have made it through without you and Jesus. I adore you all and may God get all the glory and honor from sharing this intimate part of our lives with others, in hopes they too will find hope. God bless you all with long life, peace, and joy.

I love you.

Trusting God Even When
It Doesn't Make Sense

Sometime later, God tested Abraham's faith. "Abraham!" God called.

"Yes," he replied. "Here I am."

"Take your son, your only son —yes, Isaac, whom you love so much—and go to the land of Moriah. Go and sacrifice him as a burnt offering on one of the mountains, which I will show you."

The next morning Abraham got up early. He saddled his donkey and took two of his servants with him, along with his son, Isaac. Then he chopped wood for a fire for a burnt offering and set out for the place God had told him about. On the third day of their journey, Abraham looked up and saw the place in the distance. "Stay here with the donkey," Abraham told the servants. "The boy and I will travel a little farther. We will worship there, and then we will come right back."

So, Abraham placed the wood for the burnt offering on Isaac's shoulders, while he himself carried the fire and the knife. As the two of them walked on together, Isaac turned to Abraham and said, "Father?"

"Yes, my son?" Abraham replied.

"We have the fire and the wood," the boy said, "but where is the sheep for the burnt offering?"

"God will provide a sheep for the burnt offering, my son," Abraham answered. And they both walked on together.

When they arrived at the place where God had told him to go, Abraham built an altar and arranged the wood on it. Then he tied his son, Isaac, and laid him on the altar on top of the wood. And Abraham picked up the knife to kill his son as *a sacrifice. At that moment the angel of the Lord called to him from heaven, "Abraham! Abraham!"*

"Yes," Abraham replied. "Here I am!"

"Don't lay a hand on the boy!" the angel said. "Do not hurt him in any way, for now I know that you truly fear God. You have not withheld from me even your son, your only son."

Then Abraham looked up and saw a ram caught by its horns in a thicket. So, he took the ram and sacrificed it as a burnt offering in place of his son. Abraham named the place Yahweh-Yireh (which means "the Lord will provide"). To this day, people still use that name as a proverb: "On the mountain of the Lord it will be provided."

Then the angel of the Lord called again to Abraham from heaven. "This is what the Lord says: Because you have obeyed me and have not withheld even your son, your only son, I swear by my own name that I will certainly bless you. I will multiply your descendants beyond number, like the stars in the sky and the sand on the seashore. Your descendants will conquer the cities of their enemies. And through your descendants all the nations of the earth will be blessed—all because you have obeyed me."

—Genesis 22:1-18, NLT

Contents

Preface ix

1. In the Beginning 1

2. The Birth 11

3. Waking Up 25

4. A Promise 35

5. Trials of Various Kinds 45

6. The Turnaround 59

7. Remembering the Promise 69

8. The Completion of the Miracle 79

HARP Initiative 87

Preface

THIS IS OUR STORY OF HOW A BABY WAS SENT TO CHANGE "our" world. And by our world, I mean our family, our church, our friends, our community, and, quite possibly over time, even the world. This is a story of truth, faith, brokenness, hope, perseverance, promises, the power of prayer, present-day miracles, and the very nature of Jesus.

We are a family who loves God, but we didn't truly know His complete nature. I dare say most people don't experience His fullness until you are in the belly of the whale (as in the case of Jonah from the Old Testament). When you come to your lowest point, that is when you look up to see His face and those eyes of love. Until you have seen or felt the love of Jesus, it is hard to fully explain in words to others. We will not fully know Him until we meet in Heaven, but we can become much more aware of His goodness, mercy, love, power, intimacy, and blessings like never before. It is hard to think or even consider how you could even think of having peace in the middle of pure turmoil and chaos, the peace the Bible talks about. It surpasses all our human comprehension and is a supernatural peace that comes only in surrender and times of pure disarray.

This is the story of how our family was completely shattered, broken, and then restored to a place of healing, thriving like never before. Our story of complete surrender and seeing God move and fully trusting Him to provide in the trial. Our story of faith and how we stood in the face of defeat and even death. This is how the birth of a baby boy, Levi, changed our lives forever. I pray our story touches you deep down inside. I pray you feel the presence of God as you turn the pages of this book. I pray you see the goodness of God and His mercy in between the lines and words. I pray the promise that you need jumps off the page and surrounds your heart as only God can do.

Lord,

May You use this book, this story, for Your glory. May Your presence and truth be attached to every word and page. May each reader see a glimpse of Your goodness and mercy from our testimony. Thank you, Lord, for the chance to bring You honor and share this with as many people as You see fit.

Amen.

1

In the Beginning

MY HANDS WERE SHAKING, AND TEARS STREAMED down my face as I read the two lines on the pregnancy test. Positive. I remember vividly the day I found out I was pregnant with our third child; it was not a planned pregnancy. I was scared, frightened, anxious, and worried, feeling overwhelmed and defeated. I felt like I was failing as a mother already, so how could I add one more person to be responsible for? I was living in a state of survival, as so many mothers are today. How could I take care of one more person? How could I be responsible for one more life? How could we fit one more person in our small starter home?

My mind swirled, and my heart was heavy within me with fear and what if's. The thoughts flooded my mind constantly, penetrating every aspect of my life. I literally made myself sick with worry over our future child. Here was this precious gift of life growing inside of me, and I could not even enjoy it due to my own mess and fears! All I could think about was what am "I" going to do? My attitude and my thoughts were all centered around me and not this sweet gift growing inside me. But oh, how all that changed in one moment.

Before we move forward, I want to rewind for a second and give you a little bit of our back story. My husband, Ricky, and I dated for two years before we were married in May of 2003. I was twenty-four at the time and he was thirty. A year and a half later, we welcomed our first baby boy, Graham. Five years later, we welcomed another precious baby boy, Clayton. In January 2014, we were still living in our starter home. We had made a choice to sacrifice one income so I could stay at home to raise our boys. This was an incredible blessing, but it is also not for the faint of heart. Being a stay-at-home mom is incredibly rewarding, while also being one of the most challenging things I have ever done. My husband owns his own landscaping business and at that time, he worked from sunup to sundown. By this time in our journey, our oldest was nine and our youngest was five. Our marriage had been through its ups and downs, but we had remained together, struggling like all families can do at times. We had a hard time maintaining peace in our family. We loved Jesus and loved going to church, but we were missing something that was very much needed. We were missing an intimacy with Jesus.

In February of that year, 2014, I went on a women's retreat. At this point in my life, as a stay-at-home mom, I was desperate for a change. My soul needed refreshment; to be honest, most days I struggled with happiness and fulfillment, even though I had so much to be thankful for. I had struggled with postpartum depression and guilt from my past. I had run from God for about six years as a young adult after moving out on my own. I had lived a party life, indulging in many relationships, drugs, and alcohol. I struggled with feeling forgiven or even worthy of being a parent. I felt like a failure and struggled to find my place or where I belonged. As I left for this retreat, I knew something had to change. I was desperate; my heart and soul ached within me and longed for the joy promised in the Bible. Being a Christian, saved by grace, why was I not living a life of abundance? Did God not promise us joy? I was struggling to find what His Word promised.

One evening during the retreat, I laid face down on the floor in the living room of the rental house I was staying in. I cried out to God, re-surrendering my heart and my life back to Jesus. I had become so complacent and engulfed in my own woes to even begin to think about doing anything constructive for God. Unfortunately, I was looking at all the things I was doing wrong or missing out on instead of looking at what really mattered: my family and my relationship with the One who created me. That night on the floor, I surrendered myself, my husband, and my children to the Lord, begging God to use my family and me in a mighty way. The theme for the retreat was: **Who is God? Who is He really? What does His Word say about Him?**

The two main points were:

- We must trust God's heart when we can't see His hand.

- We can't come to Him unless He draws us.

These two statements became so true to me over the next year, and I had no idea what they were foreshadowing.

The retreat speaker asked us two questions at the first evening session of the weekend:

- Where is God leading you?

- Have you surrendered everything to Him?

I asked myself these questions and began to journal what I heard God say. He showed me my weaknesses, the areas where I needed to change and where I needed to let go. He gently revealed to me that I was not to stand in the way between Himself (God) and my husband and children. I needed to let go of always trying to be right and trying to be in control when things did not go the way I wanted. I needed to trust that God is everything I need, no matter what the circumstances. God wants what is best for me and my family.

The Father also showed me that I need to trust that He loves my family, even more than I do, and that He knows what is best for them. He knows much better than I ever will. I realized I needed to surrender my marriage and my husband to Him. I could not change my husband, and I was hurting us both trying to do so. We had struggled our entire marriage to have peace, two broken people in need of healing and a Savior. In our pain, we caused each other more pain.

It amazes me how God works. How He prepares us for real life. How He prepares us for the storms, even before we face them. Even as I write this, I am in awe of His timing and His story. We each are a story being written in time, and our stories intertwine and create the most magnificent story ever. Our stories are never complete until we face death, and even then, we begin a whole new story in eternity. It takes a lifetime to write our stories, yet we want things to happen overnight. However, His timing is perfect; it just takes time to see it come to fruition.

One of the scriptures from the women's retreat was,

> *Blessed is the man who TRUSTS in the Lord, and whose hope is the LORD. For he shall be like a tree planted by the waters, which spreads out its roots by the river, and will not fear when heat comes; but its leaf will be green and will not be anxious in the year of drought, nor will cease from yielding fruit. (Jeremiah 17:7-8 NKJV)*

Oh, how I needed and desired to be that *flourishing tree* nestled beside the river!

My biggest weakness, which affects everything, is my lack of fully trusting God. I have struggled most of my life with trusting people as well, due to hurts in my past and present. I tend to put up walls between others and myself, as I expected people to hurt me and let me down, which is a sin to do. Instead, we must trust in God completely, for HE never changes and stays the same. He is the same God who parted the Red Sea. He is the same God who healed the blind and the sick. He is the same God that raised His Son from the dead. He is the same today, and He has the same power! He can do ALL THINGS! We know this. I knew this! It has been ingrained in me since I was a small child, yet still on this retreat, at thirty-four, I struggled to completely trust Him.

In all His goodness, God was preparing me for a move in my life that would propel my family into the hardest days we had ever faced in our lives. But still, in all His mercy and love, He was about to teach me how to trust Him with everything. He was about to show us all the fullness of His love and grace. He was about to show me the desperation of not knowing the outcome of my life and that of our very own child. The birth of our third son, Levi, would rip our semi-normal life off its axis and bring it slamming down. In a moment, our lives changed. Eleven years into our marriage, the birth of a baby changed every aspect of our lives in an instant.

How can anyone have peace when their child is fighting for life? Or their spouse? Or their parents? How can they have joy in situations like this? This is the difference that Jesus makes. This is when the supernatural power we gain when we are saved and filled with the Holy Spirit comes through for us. When we have a relationship with Jesus, He gives us a direct link to God and His power, and this power allows us to survive; not just survive but thrive. It awakens and stirs our souls in depths and places we never knew existed, giving us the ability to face the darkest, toughest times in our lives.

- *"Even though I walk through the valley of the shadow of death, I will fear no evil, for you are with me; your rod and staff, they comfort me. You prepare a table before me in the presence of my enemies; you anoint my head with oil; my cup overflows. Surely goodness and mercy shall follow me all the days of my life, and I shall dwell in the house of the LORD forever." Psalm 23:4-6 ESV*

- *"O LORD my God, I cried to you for help, and you have healed me." Psalm 30:2 ESV*

- *"My soul is weary with sorrow, strengthen me according to your word." Psalm 119:28 NIV*

- *"For nothing will be impossible with God." Luke 1:37 ESV*

- *"The LORD replied, "My Presence will go with you, and I will give you rest." Exodus 33:14 ESV*

- *"Truly my soul finds rest in God, my salvation comes from Him." Psalm 62:1 NIV*

- *"Yes, my soul, find rest in God; my hope comes from Him." Psalm 62:5 NIV*

I could go on and on with verses that share about the hope, rest, and strength that He offers us and gives us freely, if we will receive it. The Bible is full of them because God knew life was going to be hard and even completely overwhelming at times! When sin entered the world, pain, suffering, and even death came right along with it. The perfect world that God had created for us became difficult, hard, and even deadly. But God never left Adam and Eve in the beginning. Even after they turned their backs on Him, He never left them and still loved them unconditionally. God did not force Himself on them, because true love is never forced. He gave Adam and Eve, all of humanity, including us, a choice to choose Him or not to choose Him, loving us through our trials and sin. He made clothes for Adam and Eve in their fall and provided for them because of His reckless love for them.

Death and separation from God are our punishments for our sin. We all have sinned and fallen short of the glory of God, but He loves us so much that He sent His one and only Son Jesus to die for us (Romans 3:23, John 3:16). Jesus came to take on our punishment, our sin. Our separation from God was reversed through Jesus's blood and atonement. The blood of an innocent lamb had to be shed so the tainted, broken, and wayward humans that we are, could have a way to be with God.

Jesus came as a vulnerable, real, fully human babe. It says in *Philippians 2:5b-8 ESV:*

> ... *Christ Jesus, who, though He was in the form of God, did not count equality with God a thing to be grasped, but emptied*

himself, by taking the form of a servant, being born in the like-
ness of men. And being found in human form, He humbled
himself by becoming obedient to the point of death, even death
on a cross.

It can be hard to think of God or Jesus in this way. But He came
so we could be made whole, and He came so we could have a way
to be forgiven of our sins and have lives of fullness and abundance,
even before Heaven. This tiny babe came to save the world, cried,
and felt hunger and pain. He felt afraid, overwhelmed, and was
tempted, yet never sinned. He felt love and sadness, joy and grief,
every emotion that we have felt or ever will face. He wept and cried
out to His Father, God. He prayed and cried out so intensely *"…*
being in agony He prayed more earnestly; and His sweat became like great
drops of blood falling down to the ground" (Luke 22:44 ESV). He suffered
physical pain like no other and had faced all these things, yet He
overcame them all. This is how we find hope and comfort in Him,
because through Him, we can overcome all things too.

His power and peace can overcome anything. It can help us face
any hardship, any pain, any fear, any struggle that may come our
way. When we see our need for Him and surrender our will and life
to Him, then the same power that defeated death, raised people from
the dead, healed the sick, and parted the Red Sea comes into us. It
can cover us. It can work through us, for our benefit and for His
glory. The following is said in His Word, the Bible, *"He (Jesus) re-*
plied… Truly I tell you, if you have faith as small as a mustard seed, you
can say to this mountain, "Move from here to there', and it will move, and
nothing will be impossible for you." (Matthew 17:20 NIV). A mustard
seed is so small, so minute. But if we have only as much faith as a
mustard seed, we can do great things through Him and for Him.

So, what is faith? Faith is the complete trust or confidence in
someone or something. It is a strong belief based on spiritual appre-
hension rather than proof. How do we gain faith? How do we live
out our faith? How do we get past our fears and doubts? How do
we genuinely believe that if we speak to a mountain that it will

move? How can we speak life into a lifeless body? How can we speak healing over death and/or cancer? How do we speak boldly in the face of fear and what the world says is impossible? Is it Him inside of us? Is it us believing in the unseen?

This is faith; it is when we walk not by sight but by His Word and His power, when we accept Him as our Savior, that then we are filled with the Holy Spirit. We are filled with His power and His glory. We can speak complete and total healing over ourselves and others through Jesus's mighty name. We can do unimaginable and inconceivable things through our Lord, Jesus Christ. His power and authority, imparted to us through His blood and salvation, enables us to do even greater things than He did here on earth. That faith, that power, that glory enables us to move mountains if we truly believe, for His Word says, *"I tell you the truth, anyone who believes in me will do the same works I have done, and even greater works, because I am going to be with the Father." (John 14:12 NLT)*. And that is just what we did when our third son, Levi, came face to face with death the day he was born.

I began a relationship with Jesus when I was twelve; but as an adult, at this time in my life, I lacked true intimacy with Him. We went, as a family, to church on Sunday and Wednesday nights. We prayed at night, prayed before we ate, but still something was missing. It felt like more of a routine than a relationship with God, and I desired more. I felt like something was missing. My soul was desperate for something, for God, for Jesus. And the God of the universe was about to show me all His goodness, love, mercy, and power in the middle of a trial that felt like my life was ending. We had no idea just how much our sweet child was about to suffer, or us as we watched him fight to live.

We as humans look at the physical, seeing death, pain, and suffering as punishment, not as anything to be thankful for. His Word says, *"He has plans to prosper us and not to harm us" (Jeremiah 29:11)*. What if our prosperity in this life is not wealth? What if it is peace and joy and complete trust of our heavenly Father? What if this is God's true and perfect gift to us, but the only way to truly see this truth as such is to experience heart-wrenching pain and trials? This is what I have seen firsthand, having learned that even though I faced the hardest trial in my life, I also felt closest to God during it. I also felt the peace that surpasses all understanding through it. How could this be? Because God's Word says, "Consider it pure joy, my brothers and sisters, whenever you face trials of many kinds, because you know that the testing of your faith produces perseverance" (James 1:2-3 NIV).

Yet, how can we even begin to consider death, pain, and suffering pure joy? How can this be joy or even bring joy? Heart-wrenching pain cannot possibly bring joy to us when it immediately occurs, but it can come when we seek Jesus wholeheartedly during the pain. Joy can come when we give Him thanks in the midst of the trial.

This kind of pain I am talking about is the kind that breaks you to your core. The kind that steals your breath and makes your body too heavy to move. As it comes, it removes everything that carries no real weight of importance in life and leaves you raw and bleeding. Nothing else matters anymore, as all material things vanish. When our world was crashing down around us and shaken off its axis, nothing else mattered except for that precious life fighting to live. That little babe that was facing obstacle after obstacle to just breathe. Nothing else mattered!

This is when your heart is raw! This is when we become the most vulnerable and open to God. This is when we are at our most desperate, when all we can do is cling to Him. He is a necessity to survive, a necessity to even continue to breathe! This is the time when we must truly surrender ourselves to Him, allowing Him to reign and completely take over. This is when His peace that surpasses all understanding becomes real.

2

The Birth

NOVEMBER 24, 2014

Today was the day!! It was the day we would welcome our sweet baby boy into the world. However, I woke up that morning feeling anxious. This was our third child, so we should be pros, right? It was a scheduled C-section, my third, I knew what to expect, but something felt amiss. I felt uneasy, anxious, and fearful. In the beginning, I had questioned God if I was ready for a third child, but I was ready now to welcome this precious bundle. Medically speaking, I was considered to be of advanced maternal age at the age of thirty-five now for this third pregnancy. This had included extra doctor visits and ultrasounds, but our Levi looked healthy and so did I. But this morning, as we hustled to get in the car with our bags, the atmosphere was different. I felt heaviness, an unrest that I could not explain and could not shake. I began to pray, and a verse popped into my head. *"For I know the plans I have for you, declares the LORD, plans to prosper you and not to harm you, plans to give you hope and a future" (Jeremiah 29:11 NIV).* This verse just rolled over and over in my mind and my spirit. It became my plea as I tried to push past the heaviness and worry. My husband seemed unscathed, but I remained somber as we drove towards the hospital. I became a little desperate, so I opened my *Jesus Calling* devotional, by Sara Young, for the morning of November 24th.

The words hit my spirit like a ton of bricks. It was just the first dose of promises the Lord revealed to us during this time. I tried to push back the feeling of heaviness and fear I had. What was this that I was feeling? Was it normal anxiety for a delivery, or was it God preparing me for what was coming? Was He preparing my soul? Yes. He was reminding me of His promises, reminding me that NO matter the heartrending hardships we face, we must give thanks that He is always with us.

Even when we do not know what is going on, even then He is calling us to give thanks and to trust Him. Blind, obedient thanks? Even when we feel like all hope is lost, could He really desire or expect us to give Him thanks? Is it even possible for Him to work all things out for the good of those who love Him? Blind obedience? When we cannot see the end result, and we cannot see the good that is to come from the pain, how can we give thanks? How?

My mind raced after reading this devotional, and I tried to settle myself by praying and breathing. Yet the verse "God has plans to prosper us, not to harm us" flooded my mind and soul. I held on to that promise … prosper!!

We arrived at the hospital, and everything seemed off. The nurses were in a rush, as though they were just as overwhelmed as I was. They scurried about as they checked my vitals and Levi's. My mom arrived late with our two older boys, who had stayed with her for the night so we could arrive early for the delivery. We did not get to see our other two boys before we went back for surgery. We did not even get the chance to pray together right before they wheeled me back for delivery. We always tried to pray as a family for each other, as prayer was something that had been ingrained in me, since I was little. I had prayed all morning, but I had wanted to pray together as a couple and with our boys. It all seemed so chaotic.

Something was off; there was a battle going on that morning. One that started in the spiritual realm and spilled over into the physical. *"For we do not wrestle against flesh and blood, but against the rulers, against the authorities, against the cosmic powers over this present darkness, against the spiritual forces of evil in the heavenly places"* (Ephesians 6:12 ESV). Our physical eyes look for answers, and we try to explain in the natural world, yet so many times they cannot be answered this way.

Sometimes the answers are hidden, hidden in time, or hidden in deep intimacy with our Creator. We must search for them, but not in the way you would think. We must surrender our way and will, so His can become the only way. My will was for my son to be born perfectly healthy, full of life, but it came about a different way than I thought it should come.

The hospital staff began to prepare me for surgery, placing a monitor on my abdomen to check the baby's heartbeat. All was well in my hospital room. He, my son, physically punched the heart monitor off my belly while it was strapped across me. (He was a fighter, even in the womb.) They wheeled me back to the delivery room, and the nurses and anesthesiologist had me lean over to insert the spinal block. I felt a sharp kick in my abdomen, which startled me. It was not a normal kick. They shortly began the C-section after that. All looked to be going well, but I began to feel such heaviness on my chest. I could not breathe and began to complain because my chest felt as if it were being crushed. It felt as though an elephant was sitting on my chest.

They administered a couple of shots of ephedrine because my blood pressure began to drop, and then they pulled out our sweet boy. Unfortunately, Levi Asher was blue and not breathing. Our perfectly healthy baby, up until this point, was now lifeless. They began to suction his airways and try to revive him. During this time, I had no idea what was taking place. I could not see anything due to a blue sheet they put up during the C-section to keep the mom from seeing the procedure. However, I knew something was wrong because of my husband's actions. He would look up over the sheet and then put his head down on the table beside me. I heard no cry, only heard people moving about, and then I heard my doctor say, "How is it going over there?" No answer.

By this time, panic was beginning to creep in. I finally heard a small whimper of a cry but had no idea what was happening. No one was saying anything ... not even my husband. He did not have to ... his face and actions said enough.

After the delivery, they moved me into a recovery room. My husband stayed behind in the delivery room with Levi as they wheeled me out. I was moved into a small white, sterile room with a nurse that I had just met a couple of hours before. There was an eerie, awkward silence in the room as she watched my vitals and got me comfortable. I lay there numb. Another lady entered the room carrying a clipboard. She said, "Ma'am, I need you to sign this paperwork. We need to transport your baby to the NICU at Regional." My heart dropped ... why? What was happening? How could this be? This could not be part of the plan. How could God allow this to happen? What was wrong with my healthy baby?

I signed the papers, still not knowing the full extent of what was happening. It seemed surreal, like a sad movie. The lady left the room with the papers, allowing them to take my sweet baby away from me. I was terrified. A million things were going through my mind ... I wish I could say I stopped right then and prayed and trusted God, but I did not. I froze. I pulled back from reality. I froze in time, in fear, in doubt, and in disbelief. I got caught up in the circumstances of the fear that surrounded me. But still ... in my frailty and weakness, God provided. He moved when I could not and provided a prayer. The nurse that had silently been taking care of me asked me if she could pray with me. I said yes. She prayed and said words I could not even muster up to say. God provided.

I stayed in this small recovery room for what seemed like forever. The silence there was deafening. Finally, they wheeled me into my hospital room. This was supposed to be a time of joy and newness of meeting our sweet gift, but it was not as I had planned. It was a newness but not the kind I desired. I had never experienced something so traumatic.

My family poured into the room behind me. I do not remember what was said during this time. I was gone, retracting mentally into a reclusive state. My mind and soul were in shock, numb. The only thing I remember during this time was that everyone was looking at me with those eyes. You know those eyes that I am talking about ... the eyes that are filled with sadness and fear, but they do not really know what to say. A person's eyes can say a lot; they can reflect the soul and emotions of a person better sometimes than their own words.

The hospital room door opened and in came a metal box on wheels, a transport unit holding our sweet boy. It was a transport incubator, a mobile, enclosed unit designed to create a controlled environment for infants. It is a small stretcher enclosed in a clear box for safety. My sweet angel, whom I had carried for thirty-nine weeks, lay there lifeless, with wires coming out from all over his sweet, little body. He looked perfect with ten little toes and ten little fingers. But his life was hanging in the balance right before our eyes. They wheeled the transport unit over close to my hospital bed. This was the first time I had laid eyes on this sweet child of mine, this piece of my heart. The transport team, neo-natal nurses, opened one side of the transport unit, and I reached over to touch his sweet, small hand and fingers. How soft and smooth they were. Oh, how I longed to grab him out of that box and hold him! This could not be happening!! How could this be real? This precious baby of mine, lying there struggling to breath and survive.

My 6-foot-1-inch husband fell to his knees weeping beside my bed and the transport unit. He was broken; I had never seen this side of him. He is a tough, manly man. I have only seen him cry a handful of times, yet here he was on the floor weeping. The reality of that moment was too intense for me. I turned my sight toward my two other boys, who were five and ten at the time. They peered into this box that contained their little brother, reaching over and touching his small hand with such gentleness that it conveyed a glimpse of their sweet hearts.

How terrifying and confusing this had to be for them: Levi lay there, covered with wires, and their daddy weeping. Standing in a room full of strangers, escorting their new brother away and family members crying ... What does this scene do to a young, innocent heart? Does it not cause trauma and pain that the outward eye cannot see? These two precious boys of mine stood there, looking at their little brother, broken, perhaps even dying. Dying? How? How could this beautiful life God had planned for us be dying? This sweet babe had not even begun to live, and death was trying to suck the life right out of him. What was happening? I could not wrap my mind around the reality of the moment.

My oldest son, Graham, was weeping as well. The entire room was filled with sounds of weeping and an eerie silence. All eyes on us and Levi. My family would look at me, then back to him. No one was ready for this pain or this trial, but that is how tragedy happens. It has no boundaries or remorse, just striking at times and knocking you down. It does not care about your race or wealth. It just attacks. The enemy comes to steal, kill, and destroy. Death comes to everyone at some point; you just never expect it at the beginning of one's life. We all will face, and have faced, hard trials. And here was Levi, facing death before his life had even really begun.

This child, could this child really be mine? He was not supposed to be broken. He was supposed to be healthy and vibrant, full of life. He was supposed to be perfect, without blemish. I had prayed for that and had prayed for him since the beginning. Yet here he was, lying lifeless. What went wrong?

Doesn't God want His children to prosper and live? Yes, but then why was this happening? Doesn't God answer the prayers of His children? Yes, but here we were facing a catastrophe of significant proportions. All this transpired within thirty minutes, yet it felt like an eternity. Pain can feel as though it stops time. Our semi-normal life was completely ripped off its axis and spinning out of control within seconds. I had no control and could not fix it. I could not close my eyes and open them to see my precious baby nestled in my arms at my breast. I opened my eyes to a nightmare instead. The pain and heart-wrenching feeling in my chest was inconceivable. This precious baby, covered with wires, was mine. My precious child was broken, and I could not fix him.

The nurses and doctor talked and made us aware of all that was going on and what the immediate plan for Levi was. I do not remember much of what was said during this time. I just remember everyone was crying ... except for me ... I was numb, frozen. The pain in my chest was suffocating, an emotional, mental reality that carried physical pain with it. I touched his sweet hand only for a second before they wheeled him away to another hospital. Everyone was weeping and looking at me. I just sat there ... frozen ... numb...

Let's pause here for a moment. As I am writing this even now, this moment is still raw in my soul and thoughts at times. Like pieces of my soul are still not completely healed from the trauma that occurred that day. This kind of pain peels back everything else, every layer. Time seems to stand still, as moments like these stops everything else. Nothing else matters. Nothing. You will never forget these moments because this kind of pain leaves a mark. Wounds may heal, but they can leave scars. It imprints on your mind and your soul forever. These wounds do not heal overnight and can only be healed by Jesus.

A labor and delivery room should be filled with joy, not death. It should be filled with oohs and aahs instead of tears. It should be a room filled with family and friends visiting you to see your new gift. But our room was filled with weeping and sadness. I sat there trapped. Trapped in a nightmare with no way out. My mind raced and my heart ached, but no tears. No words could I speak. Everyone was standing around so close, yet so far away. I felt alone amid the crowd, afraid and terrified of death. I felt betrayed by God. Where was He? Was He not with me? Wasn't He supposed to protect my son and me? His words were in my heart and my mind. *"For I know the plans I have for you,"* declares the LORD, *"plans to prosper you and not to harm you, plans to give you hope and a future."* (Jeremiah 29:11 NIV). But God!!! But God!!! Was this not harmful? Death was prowling around like a lion. But why? Why God? Where are You? I felt alone. I felt confused and angry. The doubt began to creep in, and fear was not far behind. Fear showed its evil head and pushed his way through. Fear itself can cause harm if we allow it. It can cause havoc. And it was waging war in my soul and mind.

Everyone eventually left the room after some time, leaving me alone in the hospital room. Here in these times of being alone, I had to really think about what was happening. I had to think about my son fighting for his life. I know that may sound absurd, but if I did not think about it, wouldn't it go away? Would I wake up from this horrific dream? Would this pain in my chest and my stomach go away, the pain of my soul being ripped out? There are no words to describe this pain. Unless you have faced death or pain like this, you cannot fully comprehend the severity of it. The fear of losing, specifically losing a child (or a loved one), can cause such inconceivable pain. We can feel hurt for others and even mourn with them, but we cannot fully feel the degree of the pain they feel.

I think about God allowing His own Son to die for us. He died for sinful mess-ups like me. Yet we are His children as well. He sacrificed one child for all the others. He, Himself, felt the pain of death on the cross, the agony, the guilt, the anguish Jesus felt as He breathed His last breath. Jesus was fully God, separate but one. How could God not feel it? How could God have not felt each blow, each nail that pierced part of Himself, His Son? The Trinity, the three in one: the Father, the Son, and the Holy Ghost. He felt it.

When we hear someone say, "God knows how you feel," I dare say He does. He may have even a greater wound than ours. He chose to stand back as soldiers tortured His Son. He watched them as they ripped the skin off His Son's body and hammered the crown of thorns into His scalp. He could have stopped them. He could have rained down hail and brimstone and sent ten thousand angels. He could have consumed them in fire, but He did not. He sacrificed part of Himself for the greater good, for us. We can rest knowing that God is with us and loves us. He can carry us when we have suffered the unthinkable of circumstances. He can be our comfort and place of refuge when everything around us feels broken.

When I sat there alone in that hospital room, He was with me. However, I questioned His goodness and doubted His will. How could this be part of the plan? How can such suffering do any good? The pain rips away all the junk, all the stuff that does not really matter, and leaves us vulnerable, humbled, broken, and in need of repair. In need of a healer, a comforter, of God. He never left me though even if I could not feel Him at times. This is also faith, knowing He is there even when situations seem to say He is not. We can know because His Word tells us God never leaves or forsakes us (Hebrews 13:5). That is a promise, and our heavenly Father, God, never breaks His promises.

I was desperate for Him. I cried out in pain, desperation. I questioned for a time what God would do, but I did not stay there. I turned my asking into trust as I sat there alone in that hospital room. I knew the truth about my God, my Lord, having read His Word and studied it my entire life. That is the power of knowing the Word of the Lord. When we face circumstances like these, we can find hope and courage that does not make sense. I turned my doubt into believing His promises.

I lay there in that hospital room, right in the middle of God's will for my life. I was right where God planned. Oh … I know for some of us, even me at times, to think about pain and turmoil as part of His plan, is scary. However, God does not seek to cause us harm or pain. Sickness and death entered the world through sin. The bliss of no tears, no pain, no suffering in the Garden of Eden was torn away by sin and free will of man. God had planned beauty, peace, and intimacy, as well as planned, uninterrupted communion with Him in the garden.

Imagine the beauty of the garden. The beautiful garden was filled with trees and plants of all types. The warmth of the sun and perfection it must have been. (And I am assuming it had to be warm, since they were naked and walking around … lol.) Adam and Eve lived here!! They had experienced beauty and only God's presence and blessings. Then one day, satan showed his serpent self and tempted Eve and Adam into sin, and they fell prey. They took their eyes off their creator and began to doubt His voice and words. They forgot who they were, becoming distracted and losing sight of their identities. They gave into temptation, and they suffered for it. The iniquity of man's choices brought a weight of death and destruction with it, which in turn made it possible for Jesus to come save us.

We can get angry at Adam and Eve, but we are all human, and we all have sinned in some form. Yet God, in all His goodness and mercy, still created us. He loved us still, despite all the mistakes we made and all the sins we committed. He wanted, and still wants, a relationship with us. He gave us freedom of choice as well. We all have made some horrible choices yet, if we are His, He is still with us. He has never left me and promises to never leave us or forsake us. I have felt abandoned, but He was always there in my boat during the storms. During this whole trial, there were times when I would get so distracted, I could not see Him. Then there were times when I visibly saw Jesus next to Levi.

He was with me in the hospital room, as I waited while my little one suffered across town. Here I was trapped in a bed, still feeling the physical pain of delivery. The pain in my womb of it trying to repair itself. The incision pain was great from my C-section, but nothing compared to the pain in my chest at not having my baby with me. One of the hardest things emotionally I have ever experienced was walking around that hospital hallway all by myself. Getting up due to the doctor's orders and walking down the hall by all these rooms filled with babies and parents laughing and admiring their gifts. Yet, my room was empty of laughs and snuggles. My room was filled with tears, loneliness, fear, and sadness. This pain was great and could defeat a person's soul if they allow it.

Levi had been born blue from lack of oxygen. They believe he was not breathing for several minutes due to the color of his skin, as he was pulled from my abdomen. The doctors and nurses were unsure of how long he was without oxygen. They quietly worked on him, while I lay waiting in the delivery room. Waiting to hear that first cry. That first cry of a baby as it enters the world. Yet I heard nothing and only saw my husband's face when he looked over the blue sheet between my head and abdomen. He would look over and then look down and lay his head down on his hands. I knew in the pit of my stomach that something was wrong.

I heard the doctor say, "Is everything ok over there?" The nurses worked frantically on Levi, suctioning his lungs and encouraging him to breathe on his own. In the corner of the room was the incubator, where our little one struggled. It was filled with lots of movement while no one said a word. Nothing ... then I finally heard it. A feeble, weak cry ... I still weep as I write this thinking about that sound. Life hanging in the balance. A baby fighting to breathe and be heard. Life is so fragile, and we take it for granted so much. We take breathing for granted until it is a struggle to do it, and then we fight for it. After hearing that feeble cry, I heard nothing else as they wheeled me into recovery. They had quickly inserted the ventilator into Levi's small chest, and I had no clue as to what was happening.

The doctors decided to transport Levi to the NICU at another hospital in town, as they decided the best treatment was a procedure called brain cooling hypothermia. Brain hypothermia works by cooling a baby's brain to around 33°C for three days after birth. It can help reduce brain damage and improve an infant's chance of survival while reducing the chance of disability. For four days, Levi was in a medically induced coma and remained on the ventilator during this time. His head was cooled while keeping the rest of his body warm. Levi's little body was filled full of medicines and fluids.

His little body was facing an enormous mountain; a giant was screaming at him. A giant that was swearing and screaming insults of death and destruction at such a small boy. This looked like an impossible victory for him, impossible by man's views, but looking through the lens of Jesus, nothing was impossible.

After two days, I was finally discharged. I headed straight for the NICU across town to see this precious life I had carried for nine months. The second time I saw my little one, he lay in a little hospital bed still covered in wires. His body lay still except for his chest moving up and down from the ventilator. I was unable to pick him up and snuggle him close. My arms ached to hold the piece of my heart that was lying in this small cart in front of me. His blue helmet wrapped securely around his head, cooling his brain. Levi had done well so far during the time of the head cooling, remaining stable as the nurses watched over him continually.

There is no description of the helplessness you feel in moments like these, as it cannot be adequately described in words. The feeling of not being able to fix or help your child is quite overwhelming. I imagine that God felt this anguish when Jesus was tortured. He stood by and watched, holding back His hand to reach over and wipe the enemy out. I wanted to do that; I wanted to reach over and wipe this enemy of death and destruction away from my son!

I looked down at this beautiful child, and my heart ached for him. The pain and fear that I was afraid he felt, it broke me. I rubbed his little feet and hands as I wept. I pleaded with God. Prayed and called out to Jesus to come and heal him. I was simply overwhelmed at that moment. Not knowing what to do next or what the future held for us and our little one, this was brutal.

Every evening at 6:30, we would have to leave the NICU. Six-thirty was shift change, and for an hour and a half, no one could sit with our Levi. Leaving this first night was again one of the hardest, most painful memories I have had. Leaving the hospital without a baby is one of the worst feelings a parent can ever experience. An empty car seat, we had so diligently placed securely in the back of our SUV, while anticipating the arrival of our little one, was a jolting reality of the world in which we lived at that time. This kind of pain leaves wounds and scars. Deep scars that can last a lifetime if not healed by the love and power of Jesus.

The anguish of walking into our house and trudging down the hallway into an empty nursery was surreal and can leave you feeling so much grief that it hurts to breathe. I walked into the nursery, completely ready for our little angel. The clothes hanging in the closet, a crib made up and ready to hold a sleeping baby, and a recliner ready to nurse my sweetness to sleep. But instead of a recliner filled with joy, I crumbled into the seat in pure defeat. I wept and wept bitterly. This kind of pain does not even allow you to breathe at times. You feel as if you will suffocate in that moment, and the pain does not go away. It hurts so bad, there are no words to adequately describe this kind of pain. My fragile, exhausted body felt like dying. My heart and chest hurt so badly. How could I survive this pain? How could I survive if my child did not? I prayed. I cried.

I got back up after an hour and headed back to the hospital. I sat on that hard, wooden stool beside my wee one that night until I physically could not sit anymore. I sat there until my ankles were swollen. Every night that I left that hospital without my child, my heart wound would burst open. They would have to ask me to leave at 6:30, and I would weep all the way to the car. I would walk oh so slowly and drag my heavy, weighted legs through the hospital halls and down the elevator. My body felt too heavy to move. My feet felt as if they had weights attached to them. They did have not only physical but emotional weights of heaviness, fear at times, and mere mental exhaustion.

Throughout Levi's one month stay in the NICU, I began a routine that started from mere desperation and fear. I never wanted to leave Levi's side, but I knew my body needed rest each night. When it was time to leave, I would stand beside Levi's bed in the NICU, and I would close my eyes. I would picture Jesus standing on the other side of his little bed, I would visually be picturing myself picking Levi up and placing him into the arms of Jesus. The Great Physician. The Healer. The Comforter. The Great I Am. The Redeemer. The One who came to save.

I would place my precious gift into the arms of Jesus, and I would say, "Ok he is Yours." Jesus would look down at him with such love in His eyes. Oh, how He loved Levi. He adored Him, even more so than I did. I left Levi in the only arms I trusted to hold him tight and not let go. This is the only way I could leave every night because it brought me peace. I knew He could take better care of him than any doctor in the world. He was His creator, knew him inside and out. What better arms to leave him in while I went home to rest for the night than the arms of Jesus? I knew Jesus would take care of him when I could not.

3

Waking Up

FOUR DAYS AFTER LEVI WAS BORN CAME THE TIME TO BEGIN the process of rewarming Levi back to normal, a slow process to ensure the safety of his precious, little brain. This was the day of truth, the day we would see what and if he had any damage from the lack of oxygen from his delivery. This day also just happened to be Thanksgiving, November 27, 2014. As I said before, time stands still when you are in pain. Days become a blur of time. Minutes feel like years, and time feels as though it will never end. But even amid all we were facing, we were called to still give thanks, and that is what we did. Even though we were overwhelmed, we put our eyes on Jesus and thanked Him for what was in front of us. We thanked Him that He never leaves us.

Even when we cannot feel Him or see Him at times, we know the truth, and that is when He says in His Word that He will never leave us or forsake us (Hebrews 13:5). That is a promise Jesus makes to us that love and believe in Him. Trusting when we cannot see or feel, that is called faith. Believing in something that we know to be true and real, that gives hope when all seems lost. That is the beauty of being His, a believer saved by grace and by the sacrifice of Jesus.

During the entire time of Levi's trial, I turned to social media daily to post for prayer and to pour out my heart. It was a way to express what was going on inside of my soul. It was an outlet and a way to keep our friends and family informed, asking for specific prayer requests as they came up. The prayers and support we received from our friends and family during this time was over-whelming. We could feel the prayers because they helped shift the atmosphere and welcome in the miracles that occurred. Prayer works, and it is a gift for believers, an open line of communication between us and the Father. In the Bible, it says that the prayers of a righteous man accomplish much (James 5:15-16), which means that it works and stirs the heart of the Father toward His children.

This day of the rewarming process was one of those times I felt that prayer affected the outcome. This was a big day for Levi. They removed the cooling cap at 1:26 p.m. that day and then began the rewarming period; this can take from two to four hours. Thankfully, Levi's rewarming process went perfectly, and his nurse was so pleased with how he did. She said she had never seen a baby do so well! This was an answered prayer!

When a person is removed from head cooling, there is the pos-sibility of numerous side effects. One of these is severe swelling of the head and face, and Levi faced this. His face became so swollen, he was almost unrecognizable. The fluid must move down the face and into the neck. Then it must travel into the body, where it is ab-sorbed and excreted. This is very painful to watch as your beautiful baby becomes unrecognizable and misshapen.

During a vast majority of Levi's sickness and healing, I felt bro-ken in two. There were days when I felt chewed up and spit out. I have never experienced such pain like this in my life. To watch your child, suffer so greatly is insurmountably, the worst and hardest thing, next to death and losing a child, that a parent can face. When a parent watches their child suffer, whether it is in sickness, with drugs, or through depression, it can rip a parent in half.

We, as parents, want to fix, protect, and provide for our chil-dren. And when we cannot do these three simple but complex things, we can flounder. We want to take away the pain, but we are powerless. We cannot close our eyes and make it go away either, as the nightmare is real life. Anguish can be so consuming, it affects everything. This is where some people can get stuck in pain and loss. This can lead to a life of trauma and pain unless we find healing in

Jesus. Unfortunately, trauma is a demon all on its own, wreaking havoc on our minds, bodies, souls, and hearts unlike anything else. It is usually unannounced and unwarranted, but it comes with vengeance to steal, kill, and destroy. And it will do just that if we allow it.

Levi's little body, not even a week old then, went through so much. As his head began to shrink back to normal size, they kept him sedated. This helped with the pain that he could be enduring, as the fluid was absorbed into his body. This also helped keep him comfortable during this process, allowing him to rest while the body fought so hard to survive and overcome such obstacles.

The next step was to wean him off the ventilator to see if he could breathe on his own; this process was done slowly as well to ensure his safety. They did everything slowly to watch how his body would respond. After coming off the vent, they placed him on oxygen, and he began to wake up. That day, as we said his name, Levi slowly opened his eyes. It was the first time we got to see his beautiful eyes! How beautiful this sight was. Our precious child opened his eyes and looked at us. We just wept, as this was such an amazing gift.

Seeing him moving his precious, little head around for the first time and responding to the sound of our voices was an indescribable moment and such a gift amid such heaviness. This precious child had faced so much even before we could even say hello and welcome him into this world. He entered this world into the midst of trauma, chaos, and sickness.

His blood pressure struggled to regulate as they weaned him off his meds that kept him sedated, which was a lot to endure for someone so little. Watching all this transpire caused lots of anxiety and worry for us. The beeping of those machines … if you have been in the hospital or sat with someone, you know what I mean; that sound can haunt you. Seeing your child suffer can push a person over the edge. In times like these, you must wait, sit, and pray, while trusting God to move. There was nothing I could physically do to help besides stay by Levi's side and sit with him, talking to him as he faced all these ailments and complications.

We trusted God. We had to! I mean what else do you have when you are surrounded by things like this besides faith? It is a rock that your anchor holds too. Because I promise you this, if Jesus were not my anchor, my boat would have surely been capsized and tossed into the sea of bewilderment and fear. Jesus is the Great Physician and Healer. We were trusting and asking Him for a miracle. I continually declared the promise God had given me from the beginning, that He had plans to prosper us and not to harm us. I trusted Him to provide for Levi.

The name Levi means "attached to, in harmony with." This is one thing that God did early on, bringing our family closer together. He attached us closer together in harmony for one purpose, and that was trusting God completely through all of this. He brought so many of us closer to Him through this trial.

I declared that God would be exalted through Levi's story and that many would be touched. I declared that God is good all the time; even when we could not see it or know the outcome, we just had to trust and rely on Him. We left the hospital at shift change that night in good spirits, just four days after Levi's birth. He was looking well and making excellent progress. We were joyful and left hopeful. Things were looking up.

That evening, as we sat on our bed at home, resting and talking, we received a call from the hospital. When someone you love is in the hospital, you never want to see that number pop up on your phone. We answered the call, and the nurse said she believed Levi had a seizure. This was one of the possible side effects that could happen after a lack of oxygen and was not the news we wanted to hear. The nurse said they were going to start him on seizure medicine right away. We were devastated.

Our precious, little one was suffering again. Why God? The hospital staff said it could happen, saying he might have delays or even cerebral palsy. He could be greatly affected by the lack of oxygen. His brain could have endured great harm, and we would not truly know anything until it showed up physically. Only time would tell how the brain would function and what part had been affected. The hospital staff told us he had an eighty percent chance of some sort of disability or long-term side effect from the lack of oxygen he endured right before his birth. We were unsure of how long he had been without oxygen. There was about a thirty-minute window between the time they checked his vitals in the hospital room and when they pulled him from my abdomen.

My husband and I lay there on our bed after hearing the news, weeping. "God why? Please God hear our prayers!! Save our Levi!" I remember hearing God whisper, "Cassie, do you trust Me?" "Yes, Lord I do." He said, "Then give me Levi. Surrender Him to me like Abraham gave up Isaac." I began to weep as I began to walk through the story of Abraham and Isaac. The sacrifice asked of Abraham was one that no parent was willing to hear, much less be expected to fulfill. Yet Abraham had enough faith that he obeyed the one true God and laid his son upon the altar, believing that God would provide a sacrifice in his place. He remembered the words the Lord had said when He promised to bless his descendants through the birth of his son. He trusted God's Word, and the God of Abraham had provided when he was asked to give up his son.

At that moment, I did not know the outcome for Levi's life, but I believed and trusted God who had provided for Abraham and Isaac would provide for Levi and me as well. He is the same God then as He is now. I chose to have faith and believe in miracles.

I told my husband what I heard God say. We wept. I sat there and I prayed, "God, I give You, Levi. He is Yours. He was never mine. I give Him to You, whether You save him or not. I give Levi to You. I trust You to provide a ram. He is Your son, Lord. I surrender Levi to You. I put him in Your hands. Take him, Lord." I wept but with the weeping, there came a peace that God was with us and was moving. I did not know what He was up to, but I had to trust Him.

I believed in that moment He would provide. Just as He did for Abraham, He would provide for Levi and me. He would provide the healing, the resurrection, the sacrifice, the ram!! I had to cling and hold fast to the promise that He was the same God in that moment that He was on that mountain. He was and is the same God that parted the Red Sea for the Israelites to cross safely from destruction. He was and is the same God that raised His Son from the dead and defeated death. I stepped into faith, stepped into the hope of a God who answers prayers and no matter what that answer was, I decided at that moment to trust Him. Whether He took Levi home with Him or if He radically healed Him, I was going to trust God and love Him no matter the outcome.

This was a huge turning point in my life, catapulting me into another level of faith and intimacy with my heavenly Father. And with Jesus, who became so real to me that I am forever changed and indebted to Him for His unfailing, unwavering love, my pain forced me at the feet of Jesus. A place of beauty, peace, and rest. A place where I became so intimate with my Jesus that my life was forever altered.

The next morning, Levi was better. I walked into the NICU, and he was alert and opened his eyes. I stood there, rubbing his head, and just soaking in the moment. My eyes and heart could not get enough of our precious boy. I was enthralled by his beauty and life. This little man had already faced death, even before he had truly begun to live. I watched his every move and could not get enough of his soft skin. His poor head was so swollen and misshapen, but I could not take my eyes off this beautiful gift.

The nurse walked over after I arrived, and I asked her, "When will I get to hold him?" She looked at me with sad, somber eyes and said, "Today." She saw the desperation in my eyes and heard it in my plea, knowing the bond between a mother and a child, being a mother herself. She seemed to realize for the first time that I had not gotten to hold my child since giving birth. So, she carefully wrapped him up, maneuvered all the wires attached to his little body around safely, and laid him in my arms. My heart leapt as she finally placed my sweet baby in my arms on November 29th, five days after he was born, which felt like an eternity. Oh, how I breathed him in … this precious babe so delicate yet so strong. My heart ached for him and yearned to never let go. My precious Levi, I held him for hours, as long as they would let me. I did not want to let go, and they had to make me leave that night. I did not want to put him back into his little bed before the shift change, as I never wanted to let him go again. Tears streamed down my face, hitting my shirt as I laid him down.

The warmth of his sweet, little head against my chest is what my heart and body had longed for. Since before his birth, my desire was to cuddle him and speak sweet words into his perfect, little ears. There is a special bond between a mother and a child at birth when the mama gets to hold the newborn baby against her. I had missed that time until now, worried if we would bond at first. We both had been through so much.

Well, we bonded. He bonded instantly right into my heart and into my arms. That night, I left so full; Levi was doing so well. I went home, expecting things to come and waiting eagerly to be able to take our little one home for good.

The next morning, I walked into the NICU and saw Levi off all breathing assistance. I was thrilled by this, until I heard the labored breathing. He was struggling. He had been off all oxygen for twelve hours, but because he was struggling so much, they put the C-pap back on. It helped some, but he still struggled all day. He also started having a fever, which was not an indication of being in good health. It meant something was not right and could mean so many different things.

The nurses and doctors were unsure of the cause of difficult breathing. It could have been from swelling from the head and the fluid draining into his lungs, or it could have been from damage caused by the ventilator. It was a guessing game many times during his stay in the NICU as to the breathing issues and the many different ailments he faced.

Little Levi had been through so much, just lying there struggling to survive, and I could do nothing but pray for him and love him. There are so many of us who have faced situations like this in our lives. We cannot fix things in front of us, but we, as Christians, must cling to our faith, having the gift of trusting and believing in God. This gives us hope, something to hold on to when nothing else makes sense. It gives us a place to run to so we can run to the arms of Jesus. He is our constant and our companion. He is the Great Physician and Healer, our best friend if we let Him be.

We continued to have faith and pray for complete healing for our boy. They did a head ultrasound and an EEG that morning. An EEG is a recording of brain activity. During this test, small sensors are attached to the scalp to pick up the electrical signals produced by the brain. The first test looked good, but there was some background noise, which meant there could be brain damage. This was not what we wanted to hear.

This time was so exhausting, physically, and emotionally, for everyone in our family. One of my older boys caught a stomach bug during these first few weeks after Levi's birth, which caused us to be separated from both boys due to the danger of exposing Levi or us to sickness. It could have kept us from being able to visit him in the NICU, so I had to make a choice. I had to sacrifice time with one sick child to see another, which created more tension and turmoil within me. My mama heart broke, as I longed to hold all three of my boys. I longed for normalcy, and this separation caused me to feel useless, helpless, and alone at times.

There are really no words to adequately express what you feel during times like these. These times of trauma and pain will either make you or break you, build up a family or tear it down. Times like these will help a marriage grow or rip it apart. Levi's birth slammed my husband Ricky and I into each other, which was part of how God brought healing and restoration to our family through using what the enemy meant for harm for our good. We had struggled throughout our marriage to have peace, having faced some hard months in our marriage leading up to Levi's birth. Levi's birth opened our eyes to each other and to our selfishness, helping restore our hearts and love towards each other.

Dec 1, 2014, 7:29 AM

I would like to publicly thank my husband. He has been amazing through all of this. He goes at least three times a day to see our precious baby. He went when I could not and stayed with him during the day and would come stay with me at night. He gets up early every morning and goes to see him. He then goes and takes care of some work things and comes back to pick me up, and we go back. We stay till 6:30 when you must leave. He brings me home, and we eat and rest and usually he goes back by himself one more time (because I have been too weak to go back). He then comes home and sleeps for a few hours and begins the routine again. I can say that through this hardest week of our lives, I have never been more in awe of a man. My love for him has grown in leaps and bounds. I have never seen anyone pray so much for another human being as he has prayed for Levi. He has literally prayed without ceasing. I am overwhelmed by his love for our family. I am truly honored, blessed to be married to such a man. God knew before time that we would be together, and I am so thankful that he was in my plan. I love you beyond words. You are an amazing father, and I am in awe of the bond you and Levi already have. Thank you from the bottom of my heart. I love you.

I share this online post I wrote because even in the ashes, there was beauty. I share because I want to give you a glimpse of hope through trials. What God can do through pain sometimes cannot be done any other way. Life is rough and can come with force that knocks you down, but it is in those times where we see what we are truly made of. What really matters… we see the realness of who we are. We see who God created us to be.

My husband was a godsend throughout all of Levi's sickness, and I began to see just how God had designed us for each other. Trials can bring out the worst or the best in people, and this trial with Levi exposed the true love my husband had for our family. He went above and beyond for us.

Through all of this, it seemed at times my husband and I took turns being strong. One of us would be strong, and the other less strong. There were also times when we were both weak, but that was ok because we had our faith, and we had God, Jesus, and the Holy Spirit. We had our family and thousands of people praying for us. Prayer changes so much, stirring up the heavens and the very heart of God our Father. He wants us to talk to Him, hears our cries. And when two or more gather in His name, He is with them (Matthew 18:20).

By the first of December, we had thousands of people praying for Levi. People literally were praying for him all over the world, reading his updates online. Prayer changes things and is our gateway straight to God. When we are His and surrender completely to God, confessing with our mouths that Jesus is Lord and believe, then we become children of God. One of the gifts He gives us is prayer, where we can talk directly to God. In His Word, it says He hears the prayers of the righteous, and they are full of power (James 5:16). This power is what we stood on as we prayed and cried out for Levi; it is what we believe in and relied on. We had faith that it could change Levi's outcome; it could save his life, as the same power that raised Jesus Christ from the dead lives in us as believers. Prayer changes things. I have seen it happen.

> *You can pray for anything, and if you have faith, you will receive it. (Matthew 21:22 NLT)*

On December 1st, my husband got to hold his third son for the first time. Pure joy and love flooded his face holding Levi. They had already bonded, but this moment sealed the deal. My husband had been there with Levi for the first few days of his life, whispering into his ears all the love he could. He would rub his feet and hands, all the while telling him how much he loved him. He would stroke his small forehead and let him know he was not alone. Their bond was formed early on and remains just as strong and intimate today.

4

A Promise

AFTER SURVIVING BREATHING ON HIS OWN, THE NEXT feat Levi faced was eating from a bottle, as he had been on a feeding tube since shortly after birth. They assumed, and pretty much assured us, he would have issues sucking due to possible brain damage and missing that initial time of nursing right after birth. We prayed and asked our family and friends to cover Levi in prayer for this situation, and yet again another miracle from God occurred! He took the bottle with ease and immediately latched on, doing amazing the first time at feeding! We were beside ourselves with excitement. If he kept on this road of recovery, then we would be home quickly!

But then came the second day of feeding, and this day went downhill very quickly. I was holding my sweet baby and feeding him. As the day progressed, I could feel his small body become clammy and noticed he became mottled. His complexion had become pale, and the mottling over his body grew as the day went on. The nurses and doctors believed that these were signs that his body was stressed and possibly had been fighting off an infection. His breathing became very rapid and labored, staying that way even after they stopped the feedings.

This was a huge setback and terrifying to watch. Something was very wrong with our Levi, as he struggled to breathe and eat. I spoke to the nurse about it, and she immediately became alarmed. I could see the concern in her face as she began to check him out very closely. His vitals were constantly being monitored with multiple sensors, but his body showed definite signs of struggle quickly. She began to listen to his lungs and noticed how hard his heart was pumping. He was struggling to breathe, and his little chest raised up and down with each breath violently. You could see his heart literally beating against his chest and ribs.

Urgency filled our little section in the NICU. Nurses ran around, calling the doctor back in, who had just stepped out for dinner. He came back in immediately and saw the drastic decline in Levi's health. Right away, he made a call to the heart specialist from another hospital. Levi was much sicker than they had originally thought, and we did not know if he would make it through the night. His heart was struggling so hard and beating with such force! Levi's body was so sick, and we had no clue as to why. We were yet again devastated by this news.

As usual, I had to leave for shift change that evening, unsure of what was happening. I was unsure if I would see Levi again, alive. Everything within me did not want to leave him. The sight of so many nurses and doctors surrounding him as I was told to leave was terrifying. I wept and had to force myself to leave. When I got in the car, my husband and I cried out in urgency to God. "God!! Levi was doing so well. What is happening now? Please God, we need You!! Help us, help our sweet boy! Lord, You have plans to prosper Levi and not to harm him. We trust You to provide."

They ran multiple tests. His blood pressure was very high, and they could not figure out why. They fed him fluids because he was lacking a certain kind in his body, but this was one of the many unknowns during Levi's sickness. It was as though we could never get clear answers from anyone, as though the battle over his sweet body was of greater magnitude than just physical sickness. This battle was of a deeper spiritual nature, as the enemy came to steal, kill, and destroy his life, and we had to fight for it. We had to fight a battle in the spiritual realm of prayer and watch it spill over into the natural world, as answers and miracles would take place and develop.

Throughout Levi's sickness, God gave us sweet gifts of promises over Levi. Friends of ours had remarkable, supernatural visions of Levi being made whole and promises spoken by the Father through them over his healing. These promises gave us hope and helped build our faith. I truly believed with my whole heart that God was going to completely heal Levi. Although I knew this, my flesh was at times still weak, but I never stayed in this place of defeat for long. I would not allow myself to, as my son needed me to speak life over him. God has grace for us in times of trials. He wants us to fall into His arms, but He also wants us to grab hold of His promises and use them to change the world around us. He has given us the ability to speak life into death. We must do this even when we feel we cannot go on; we must use His strength when we have none. We can do ALL things THROUGH Christ, who gives us strength.

I want to say that during those first nine days of Levi's life, my husband and I were broken to our core. My prayer, throughout my life, had always been that God would use me and make me stronger each day. And so many times, God accomplishes this through allowing trials in our lives. His Word says, *"Consider it pure joy, my brothers and sisters, when you face trials of many kinds, because you know that the testing of your faith produces perseverance" (James 1:2 NIV)*. God is much bigger than any trial we face. He created the heavens and the earth, as well as you, me, and our little Levi. He had Levi in his hands, and we trusted Him to completely heal him.

Ricky and I had completely surrendered Levi over to God just as Abraham did with Isaac. Remember that Abraham had trusted God to provide, in one way or another, and because of that, God did great things through both Abraham and Isaac. God had something huge for Levi and our family, I believed. Even at only nine days old, God had already used this sweet babe to reach hundreds, possibly thousands, of people and pull them closer to Himself.

However, even though we had strong faith, I still was human, and my mama heart faced yet another intense jolt with Levi's health. It felt as though my heart had been physically ripped out of my body and left open. The burning and pain that I experienced is unlike anything I had ever encountered. Death and sickness can leave a sting, a mark. "Father, how can You allow this precious baby to continue to suffer so greatly? Abba!!!! Where are You?!! Do You hear my prayers? Are You still there?" I cried out in anguish.

Many will say we should not question God, but He wants all of us to talk to Him. Sometimes we are messy, and sometimes we act out. Sometimes we question God and question why our lives are happening the way they are. And that sometimes is ok. God wants to hear our cries and wants us to have a relationship with Him. That means the good, the bad, and the ugly. He wants all of it. He wants to know our hearts, so we must talk to Him. We must tell Him our hurts and our concerns.

But then, we just can't keep screaming at Him. We can't stay angry or bitter; we must listen to His voice. We must sit still and listen to His response. He is there and never leaves us or forsakes us. Sometimes He will hold His answers back to our prayers until the right time, so we need to move from questioning to listening. We must trust that He is good all the time and that He will work things out for the good of those who love Him (Romans 8:28). And when we ask and sit and listen, then the answers will come, and they did... Just not always when or how I wanted them to come.

> *And we know that in all things God works for the good of those who love him, who have been called according to his purpose. (Romans 8:28 NIV)*

A pediatric cardiologist, from a nearby hospital, came into the NICU and sat at the nurses' station that evening and read Levi's charts, looked him over, and determined his heart was enlarged. They did not yet know the cause, but they began treating him with blood pressure medicine to strengthen his heart and let it rest, hopefully allowing it to return to normal size. The hospital staff and cardiologist had little answers, so they treated the symptoms the best they knew how to for the time being.

My heart was so heavy, even though I knew the promises of God's Word. Promises of hope and a future. He has plans to prosper us and not to harm us, so I knew He could heal Levi. I believed He would. I anointed Levi with oil and read scripture over him. Every day through this trial, I continued to turn to social media to pour out my heart, asking for prayer for specific trials that came up each day. The continued response I got was overwhelming.

Our daily prayer was, "God, we claim that You are the healer of all diseases and ailments. We claim this for Levi. God, we send out this prayer in the authority of Your name that it will not come back void but will complete what it is meant to do, and that is to bring healing to Levi. God, You are good, and You know the desires of our hearts. We ask you to give them to us. AMEN."

These prayers changed us, as our urgency and desperate prayers instilled such a dependency on the Father and Jesus like never before. I believe that these prayers changed Levi's outcome, and it changed our lives. It didn't feel like an obligation but a necessity to reach out to God; it gave us strength to face each obstacle. The power that comes with intense surrender to God and complete dependence on Him is supernatural, unexplainable in words. The peace that only Jesus can give is unfathomable until experienced.

During this time, I literally felt every emotion (anger, fear, despair, overwhelmingness, brokenness, defeat), but I also felt peace like I had never experienced before and had never experienced God like this before. The brokenness, the ripping away of all distractions and worldly things, leaves you fully vulnerable and aware of God's presence unlike anything else. Even though this was the hardest thing I have ever experienced in my life, it was also the closest I had ever been with God at that time.

Throughout Levi's stay in the NICU, his nurses felt like angels in the flesh. They fought for our Levi and helped us so much in various ways. God sent earthly angels throughout all of Levi's trials. I know He sent heavenly angels to protect our Levi, but He also sent people to stand in the gap for us and him. They would come at the perfect time, His timing, and would cover us in prayer, bring us dinner, pray with us, send us messages, just come cry with us, and be there when we didn't know what we even needed. We didn't know but God knew. We were so blessed during this time with so much support from our family, our friends, our church, and even complete strangers. It's so important to have community because it is in times like these that you don't want to do life all alone ... you can't.

The next morning, the hospital staff did one of the first MRIs of Levi's brain. We would have to wait a day or two for the results of this scan. His blood pressure continued to be high and unstable, and the medicine was not working to lower it or get it regulated. His breathing remained rapid, and he was still slightly mottled. Levi's little body was under so much stress from so many things, and we continued to have no clue as to what was truly happening. He suffered so much physically. They pricked his little feet so much to draw blood every day, multiple times a day; his sweet feet still bear the scars, with his heels covered in small, white lines. Battle scars.

The next several days following this time were completely overwhelming, filled with obstacle after obstacle. Again, we felt bewildered at times, but we continued to hold onto our faith. We had to; it was the only thing that was true and sure. We felt as if we were back to square one many times in Levi's progress, taking two steps forward and three steps back. It was a constant battle of back and forth throughout the first part of Levi's life. December 5th was a hard day. It felt like giant after giant was screaming at our little boy.

Thankfully, during this time, my faith and intimacy with the Father continued to grow. I began to experience God's presence so strongly, and the peace that I felt even throughout the turmoil was only from God. It was supernatural; it was that peace the Bible talks about, the peace that surpasses all understanding. It is peace that doesn't make sense to the world or the reality that you are facing, but it really supersedes the circumstances you face.

Many believe in God but very few truly have a deep, intimate relationship with Him. Ask yourself these questions: Do you really know Him or is He just someone you shoot prayers to every now and then? Is He someone you call out to only when trouble comes knocking? Is He someone you pray to as you bless the food each day, or is He someone you communicate to continuously throughout the day?

I challenge you to really ask and answer those questions yourself. I don't want you to do this out of condemnation or feeling guilty, but out of urgency and dependency on knowing who your heavenly Father really is and what He really desires from you. Has there ever been a moment in your life when you have surrendered your life to God through Jesus? We must choose Him. God gives us free will, not forcing His way or His love on us. He offers it freely. We must choose it, choose Him. When we do this, God gifts us with peace like no other. I cannot explain in words how this peace feels, but it is a physical sensation that feels like your body absorbs it. Like every atom in your body is at peace. I mean, it is like a state of wholeness that seems so right.

There is no way I would have been able to have faced what I did without God, Jesus, and the Holy Spirit. The roller coaster you feel like you are on during times of trauma and trials is simply unreal, while the times of peace would be jolted by bouts of pain and sadness. The pain and agony my heart felt at times as I watched our tiny babe struggle to breathe every breath, the insurmountable number of medicines his small body took in, all the blood they drew from all over his body, all the tests they ran, all the nights I went home without a baby in my arms. How can a human being as small as him go through all that he has been through and survive? The overwhelming pain I felt each day as I left his bedside and walked out the door for the night ... there are no words to describe this pain. This type of pain cannot be overcome by things of this world but only through the supernatural power of Jesus. I could not have faced that without this peace and help from my heavenly Father.

There is a saying that God does not give you more than you can handle ... I believe this is untrue. Watching my child suffer and possibly die was too much to handle. Those who have lost a loved one ... that is more than our human hearts can withstand ... BUT through Him, with His supernatural strength and peace, we can overcome the pain. We can make it. We can believe.

This life is full of trials, making us turn to Him and rely on Him. This is how you survive and even thrive after facing loss and pain. This is how He gets glory and honor through our lives and how others see the goodness and greatness of God. He does allow us to face more than we can handle. But ... it is so we will turn and be solely dependent on Him, showing His glory and goodness. Does everything always turn out well and the way we want them to? No, but through His love and mercy, we can overcome if we remain in Him. He promises to bring good and work things out for the good of those who love Him.

> *Each time he said, "My grace is all you need. My power works best in weakness." So now I am glad to boast about my weaknesses, so that the power of Christ can work through me.* (2 Corinthians 12:9 NLT)

The results from the MRI came back, revealing that Levi had endured two mini strokes. They believed that one occurred before birth and one right at birth. The one after birth probably occurred when he was without oxygen or possibly as a side effect of the head cooling. The hospital staff ran more tests to see if the true culprit could be determined, if there was an underlying condition that needed to be addressed. We continued to pray for answers and for healing.

After several days of struggling to breathe, with his heart becoming enlarged, they decided to put Levi back on the ventilator to help his body rest. His heart and liver both had become enlarged. The doctor and nurses were not sure of the reason yet, but they treated the symptoms hoping to fix it with meds and nitro oxide. They tried this method to hopefully help lower Levi's blood pressure and reduce the size of his heart. The hope was that within 24 to 48 hours, his heart would shrink back down to normal size.

I couldn't understand what God was doing and why He was allowing Levi to suffer so much and face so much sickness. But I chose to trust His goodness and continue to pray and ask for healing. I placed Levi in Jesus's arms, over and over again, in prayer and every evening envisioning myself handing him over, knowing that He promised to take care of him. So, I trusted His Word and continued to declare it over him ... He has plans to prosper us and not to harm us.

As I left Levi that night, I was physically exhausted. I felt God's peace, but I also felt the fear of death staring at me. I was so broken and afraid I would not see my baby alive again. Levi was so sick. My feet were so heavy; they felt weighed down by a ton of bricks. It literally felt like someone had tied cinder blocks around my ankles, and I had to drag them along with me everywhere I went. I left for shift change that night with an extra slow, heavy walk down the hall to my husband, who was waiting for me outside. He was just getting through with work for the day and was waiting for me in the circular drive, in front of the hospital for drop-off and pick-up.

I shuffled my feet, which were laden, heavily burdened, as I walked to the elevator and down to the circle at the hospital. My body felt like it could give out on me at any second. The weight I felt inside my heart and mind overwhelmed me. My physical body was exhausted. As I walked, I cried and wept. I cried out to God in desperation, "Lord, this child is Yours. God, heal him! Please God, heal him! Your scripture says You have plans to prosper him and not to harm him. Plans for his future. God help us. Help him! I don't understand what is going on. Please help us."

As I walked outside, I felt like I was physically drowning. I opened the door and slowly climbed into the truck with my husband. I couldn't do anything but cry, as I felt like we were back to square one yet again, back on the vent and in a sedated coma ... Lord, WHY??? I felt lost, frozen, exhausted, broken, and defeated in that moment.

But ... but then came another promise from God. As Christmas music played softly on the radio and tears ran down my face, I heard the Holy Spirit speak ever so gently. The song playing was Brandon Heath's song, "The Night before Christmas." The Holy Spirit highlighted, "the night before Christmas," to me. It was like these words stood out to me and stirred my spirit. Then the Holy Spirit whispered to me, "Levi will be home the night before Christmas. He will come home on Christmas Eve." Tears filled my eyes and flowed down my cheeks, even more so, spilling onto my shirt ... I was overwhelmed and in awe.

"Lord, am I hearing You? Am I hearing You correctly? Christmas Eve? How? But God ... but God, he is so sick. They have said possibly months of hospital stay if he makes it. The doctors are baffled right now. They don't even know why he is so sick. How can this be? How will he be able to come home in a couple of weeks?" These questions rolled around in my head and my spirit.

BUT THEN ... after my many questions came hope!! In came the promises of God!! I began to pray and speak into that promise from God. It gave me new hope, and hope is HUGE at a time when your circumstances scream defeat and even possible death. Our reality, mental state can be so frail and ready to give up when we lose hope. Hope is what gets you through each day. Hope for healing, hope for another day. This was a shift for me!! This whisper from Heaven, this promise gave me a new fire to pray for Levi and gave me a promise from the mouth of my Father to my spirit! That still, small voice sounded like a trumpet to my soul!

This promise brought light into my darkness and gave me something to stand on. I knew His Word and His promises, but this was a secret word, a prophetic word from Him to me. A word that carried the promise of Levi's future in it.

> He uncovers mysteries hidden in darkness; He brings light to the deepest gloom. (Job 12:22 NLT)

God brought light to my darkness, Jesus. He gave me the gift of hope.

5

Trials of Various Kinds

WHEN YOU FACE SO MANY TRIALS, ESPECIALLY BACK-to-back, your very existence becomes somewhat shattered. The physical body at times wants to shut down and sometimes gives up. Life is too much to handle at times, and this trial for Levi, watching my child suffer in such a way, knowing that death was possible … this was too much for me to physically handle, day in and day out. I was exhausted and broken at times and so ready for normal. I was ready for life to be back the way it was before the trial. But God, through His strength in us, says we can do all things through Him (Philippians 4:13).

He is how we can do it; He is how we can face the next day, the next obstacle. He is our strength when we have none and our refuge in times of trouble. God is the very breath in our lungs when we feel as though we can't even breathe and how we face times of uncertainty. He is how we look different to the world in times of trials and is who makes us stronger, picking us up when we are too tired to walk. He is our source of life.

Sometimes He allows us to walk through trials in life so we will be dependent on Him. Well, this was one of those times in my life. I became so dependent on Him for everything. He was my source of hope, well for all of us. He helped us to survive and, come out thriving after this trial for Levi.

"You intended to harm me, but God intended it all for good. He brought me to this position so I could save the lives of many people. No, don't be afraid. I will continue to take care of you and your children." So, he reassured them by speaking kindly to them. (Genesis 50:20-21, NLT)

December 6th brought a new challenge, a new trial. Levi's little body needed a blood transfusion, as the amount of blood that had been drawn from his precious, little body for tests was too much. His small heart could not keep up. We again reached out and asked for prayer over this specific situation to our online support, asking everyone to pray that he would respond well to the transfusion and that his body would not reject the new blood. God answered that prayer, as his body accepted it perfectly. He had a rosy, pink complexion when I arrived that next morning, looking absolutely perfect.

His CBC, which is a complete blood count used to detect a wide range of issues, however, was a different story that day. His CBC was like a roller coaster ride, going up and down and all around it. Every day it would be different; one day, it would be better and then go back up the next. It was a constant barrage of results and info during his time in the NICU. A CBC test measures several components and features of your blood, including red blood cells, white blood cells, hemoglobin, and hematocrit. This test can help detect a variety of disorders, including infections, anemia, diseases of the immune system, and blood cancers. His CBC numbers continued on a roller coaster ride, for most of his time in the hospital, as the numbers would reflect the fluctuation of his health. This was in part to how sick he really was and all the obstacles his small body was facing.

Everything at this point in his journey was improving, except for his blood pressure and CBC. His blood pressure continued to rise, and the doctors could not determine the cause. We continued to have so many unanswered questions and began to ask for specific prayers yet again to be answered.

I felt a very strong urgency to ask for prayer over the specific challenges we were facing. At this point in Levi's journey, we asked for prayer for his heart and liver to be returned to normal size. We asked for protection over his lungs from pneumonia from the ventilator and for all infections to be healed. We prayed and asked for prayer over his brain, that he would have no long-term side effects from the strokes or side effects from the lack of oxygen at birth. The list of obstacles that Levi was facing seemed gruesome and overwhelming, but they were not for God. Nothing is too big for God!

The waves of emotions and feelings that you experience through a trial like this seem devastating at times. Things can change at the drop of a hat, and we all know that our lives are never guaranteed. But the hope and peace we continue to find in our faith with God, that is the anchor, the anchor that can keep your boat from sinking or drifting far out from the shore.

> *This hope is a strong and trustworthy anchor for our souls. It leads us through the curtain into God's inner sanctuary.* (Hebrews 6:19 NLT)

Even though Levi had done incredibly well with his transfusion, I was flooded with words of sickness and defeat from the "what ifs" that could happen. During this time, I began to get frustrated with God about Levi's status and progress. I was wanting things to advance at a much speedier rate. Questions swirled in my mind, things like, *why are we not seeing any big changes in Levi? What is causing this? Why is his blood pressure still up* ... and so on. I began to worry and searched Google for answers. Do you see what I was doing? I was picking Levi up out of Jesus's arms, beginning to worry and try to find answers myself, instead of trusting God's timing and His ways.

I was sitting in my chair in our little NICU area. It was not a regular room with walls and a door; it was an area enclosed only by thin curtains. Curtains don't hide noises, and they don't give much privacy when you need to weep. I was so forlorn this day because I had taken my eyes off the Father and got stuck in all the complications that I could barely move. I literally had to make myself walk to the pumping room, for nursing mothers, in the back of the NICU. I ached all over and was literally making myself sick. I was focusing on the issues at hand instead of the One who promises hope.

The weightiness of the fear of the unknown, and the known, took its toll. I began to cry out to God in that little pumping room. "LORD, I feel useless today. I can't even pray. What should I do?" I wept. "Lord, I am sorry I have begun to worry and fear. Forgive me. I lay these fears at Your feet, and I put Levi back in Your arms because I'm doing no good. Lord, I trust You to heal him. Heal him."

I slowly made my way back to Levi's bedside and began to pray over him and read my Bible and quote scripture over him. Around 3 p.m., my parents brought me lunch. The nurse came out to the waiting area as I was eating and said they were making an echo of Levi's heart. An echo is an ultrasound scan that looks at the heart and nearby blood vessels. It is used to check the structure of the heart and vessels to see how the blood flows through them and can detect heart damage or heart failure. I began to cry, and my dad began to pray as well as my mom. A lady across from us in the waiting room, a grandmother to a child also in the NICU, heard my cries and prayers. She asked if she could pray for us, and I said yes. She prayed a beautiful, precious prayer, which blessed me deeply. We prayed for good results. At four o'clock, a group of friends from our church came and prayed over us; this also meant so much to me and was yet another time when the Lord provided earthly angels. That's at least what I call them. They were the people who supported us, encouraged us, and prayed when we needed it the most.

I completely believe in the scripture that when two or more are gathered in His name, He hears their prayers (Matthew 18:20). There is power when we come together in unity after the same thing. After all this prayer and this day of heaviness, God showed me grace and showed up in a huge way for Levi. His echo showed that his heart was normal, showing no hypertension in the lungs or heart…

What??!! Just two days ago, his heart was enlarged and pumping hard. In two days... Two days!!! It had returned to normal size. His lungs were clear of hypertension. God had performed a miracle right before our eyes, and I was ecstatic!

They had to begin to wean him off the ventilator because he was getting too much oxygen. They had to lower his dose of nitro oxide because he was doing so well. His blood pressure was also down and staying stable. God showed up, big this day! Even during all the chaos, God came through.

Many times, we forget that God is in control. Many times, we try to control and manipulate things to turn out the way we want, but if we allow God to do His will, there is rest for our heavy, worn-out souls. There is healing for us, and there was healing for Levi. I know God's timing is perfect because He has a plan, a plan to prosper us and not harm us. We often want to hurry the process up, but if we stop and sit with Him, throughout trials, then that is where the growth within our souls can happen. That is what He means by prosper. God means to raise us and prepare us for Heaven. This earthly life is but a training ground for what is to come, so we must choose to trust Him! We must rely on Him and allow Him to work for us, even when we feel like giving up. He is our source.

I believe our prayers, as believers, turn the Father's heart toward His children. He wants us to ask. Many times, in scripture, the Lord tells us to ask Him. "Ask, and you will receive" (Luke 11:9). Does this mean that we get everything we ask for? No, we don't. But we are still led to ask Him. He is our Father, and He desires us to be whole. He desires for us to have an intimate relationship with Him, and praying is our communication with Him, us simply talking to our Father who created us. It does not have to include fancy words or terms; but only us sharing our hearts, fears, and dreams with our Father, asking Him for our heart's desires. We should not always do the talking though, as we must take time to be still and listen to Him speak. If we ask Him, He will teach us how to pray and what to ask for: our needs, our desires, and for others' needs as well. He will show us His desires so that when we ask, we ask for what pleases

Him because our desires will reflect His heart because we heard it directly from Him. He is not a genie in a bottle, but He is a Father who loves His children and desires them to be healthy, whole, and full of life. However, sometimes those things are only found on the other side of a trial or pain. Sometimes we must walk through the valley of the shadow of death to get to the mountain top of victory, rest, and resolution.

We continued praying and asking God to show up in big ways for Levi. We continued to pray for his white blood count to be drastically back to normal and for whatever infection that was causing his CBC to be exposed and completely removed. We prayed for his breathing to continue an upward slope. We were praying and believing to have our baby home for Christmas.

Do you see the trend here? God is a relational God because He wants a relationship with us. Does He know all things? Yes. Can He move without us asking? Yes. But does He wait on us to ask? Sometimes, yes. We see throughout scripture that God is all knowing and in complete control in Heaven and earth, but many times, we don't understand the way He operates because He moves in mysterious ways. This is unbeknownst to man unless given revelation from God Himself. He encourages us to have a relationship with Him by engaging with us through many different outlets. One way is prayer and communication with Him about our lives and trials we face. He shows up in mighty ways after and when we pray. In scripture, it says,

> *So, I say to you: Ask and it will be given to you, seek and you will find, knock and the door will be opened to you. For everyone who asks receives, the one who seeks find, and to the one who knocks, the door will be opened. (Luke 11:9-10 NIV)*

Other times, He just shows up without us even uttering a word because He is working all things out for our good. We must rely on His Word, His ways, His love, and His will. Again, we must trust Him fully, no matter what is taking place in our lives.

God's Word says we have not because we ask not (James 4:3), because many times we ask from wrong motives that don't align with His will. We must ask and share our hearts with Him because He wants to hear from us. He wants to give us good gifts and wants to build us into sanctuaries for Him and His presence. He gave us prayer as a gift and a weapon; it's our way to communicate with our Father. It's us talking to our dad and sharing our hearts and how we pour out our emotions in healthy ways, stirring the Father's heart toward us. So, every day, I would pray and ask for it all, every detail, for Levi's life. And over the next several days and weeks, God continued to leave us in awe. Even in my weakest moments, His presence would surround me. God never failed us, ever. He never left us.

On December 8th, we got more favorable news about Levi!! They made plans to begin weaning him completely off the ventilator and nitro oxide the next day. As long as his gas levels stayed good, they would proceed to remove it completely. They also began to wean him off seizure medicine because they had seen no seizure activity on the EEG or in his actions. His white blood count had come down to 30 from 36, though it still needed to lower more to be considered normal, which is between 10 and 20. His inflammation number also needed to go down from 3.2 to .4 or so.

Levi also had a scheduled eye check-up on that Wednesday, because the part of his brain that was affected by the strokes was his occipital lobe, which affects the eyes. We were praying and believing that his eyesight would be completely normal and that no damage had occurred to the nerves since his brain had endured such trauma. His blood pressure was also continuing to respond well to the medicines and remained stable. We were so overjoyed at his progress and so hopeful.

The next morning, I walked into the NICU, and sweetness was sucking his pacifier. I was overjoyed. There was no ventilator! His white blood count was also down to 17!! His inflammation rate had gone up to 4.7, which was not good, and his platelets dropped. His blood pressure was 95/64. But overall, he was looking and doing much better.

That day, sixteen days after his birth, I finally got to hold my baby skin to skin, something I had missed at his birth. My arms ached to be able to hold my sweet, little boy so close. They call this cradling skin to skin, kangarooing ... it was wonderful. My precious baby was next to my heart. Oh, how precious Levi was. We rocked and snuggled all day.

Children are precious gifts from God. Levi didn't come wrapped the way I would have picked, but if he had come without a trial, would I be so thankful for these moments? This gift of Levi and his trial ripped my heart in two but caused me to cling to God more. It caused me to reevaluate my life and to be thankful in times of complete chaos. God took a baby, broken and sick, and let his story, his life, change and impact my life and hundreds, even thousands, of others.

If you're reading this, then God has used Levi and his story to touch your heart. I pray it draws you closer to Him, to God. He did the same with Jesus. He sent Jesus as a baby, and He lived an ordinary life ... without glamor or riches as kings should have, but instead, He used Jesus and His life to heal us, to remove our sin, and to change our hearts. These gifts don't look like regular gifts. Our gift looked broken but what if, from God's perspective, these gifts were game-changers, destiny-aligners, and a way for the Lord to touch places of our hearts that could not be touched any other way? What if He had to break into our hearts to fully envelope them and really reach the place He needed to reach?

These gifts are beautiful, raw, painful, and overwhelming, yet utterly beautiful when complete. And what if being broken and poured out touched more lives in the meantime? What if being broken and mended brought growth and strength? What if God's plans of prosperity looked different than ours? His ways are higher than ours, complete and enduring. His ways contain things we can't see here on earth, or at least not until the trials are over. Consider it nothing but joy ... nothing but JOY?

*Consider it nothing but joy, my brothers and sisters, when-
ever you fall into various trials. Be assured that the testing of
your faith [through experience] produces endurance [leading
to spiritual maturity, and inner peace]. And let endurance
have its perfect result and do a thorough work, so that you
may be perfect and completely developed [in your faith], lacking in nothing. (James 1:2–4 AMP)*

He can use all things, good and bad, to work together for the
good of those who love Him.

As parents, we were so proud of Levi. God had created him to
be such a strong boy, and he was born a fighter. God's power gave
him strength to endure so much. Levi was a miracle. His very existence was a miracle, but his life and what he physically had walked
through since birth, most people would not have survived, but God.
We continued to believe that God was completely healing our little
Levi, and we knew the prayers of so many were making a difference.

Levi continued to improve, as his breathing was becoming more
and more normal. He had a blood test come back abnormal, so they
repeated it. Unfortunately, his inflammation rate continued to rise,
even when almost everything else looked like it was getting better.
The team of nurses and doctors could not figure out what was causing this to happen. His platelets also had dropped. At one point, they
thought he could have a yeast infection from all the antibiotics. They
believed it could also have been due to the stress his small body had
endured since the beginning of his life. We prayed again for this specific trial to be healed and brought to fruition through Jesus's hand.

Our prayers for Levi's eyesight were answered, and we received another miracle in that his eye exam showed completely normal activity. The doctor said everything looked like it should, and
she could see no signs or ramifications of the strokes in Levi's eyesight! This was a huge praise report!! The Father had protected his
beautiful, little eyes! We were again ecstatic from this news and gift!

That evening, Levi's PICC line stopped working; the PICC line,
at this point, was in his scalp. His PICC line was used to administer

all his medicines at this point of his journey. This had been simply horrible to watch. The nurses had to find a vein in his scalp to insert the IV line. His tiny arms, hands, and umbilical line had all been used, and the scalp was the next area to try for a vein, as they were running out of places to insert the PICC line. His body was small, and he literally had been poked and prodded all over.

Watching the nurses stick the needle into his tiny, little scalp was painful to watch. The pain he must have felt... Y'all ... this baby went through it. I mean he went through it. He was poked by a needle so many times... The pain as an infant that he had to endure and not be able to understand why this was happening. To not be able to explain to him the purpose of all these procedures ... this overwhelmed my mama heart. They had to continue to move the line to ensure that it worked properly and to keep it from becoming infected. His PICC line had developed phlebitis, which means the vein was swollen and inflamed. We had prayed that whatever was causing his inflammation rate to continue to rise, to be removed or resolved, and I believe this was the answer to our prayers.

The next day was another hard day to experience as a parent. Levi cried a lot and acted as if he was in severe pain. We believed his belly hurt. We assumed he was hungry, so they decided to attempt to feed him just a small amount. He did not respond well. His oxygen rate dropped, and his rapid breathing returned. This was devastating and another huge setback. He needed to eat to get stronger, but his body was not ready to eat and breathe at the same time. This was a huge factor in determining his time frame to be released to go home and, let's be honest, his very existence depended on it. This was so disheartening to me, as I was so ready for my sweet baby to come home.

My two older boys had only seen their little brother once in his short life, and that was in the transporter leaving Mary Black Hospital, where I had given birth to Levi. Children were not allowed in the NICU, and this was very hard for them. As a child, days and moments alter your life very profoundly ... and this affected each of our boys differently. My middle son pulled away and didn't fully understand what was happening. Our oldest son broke emotionally and became angry with God. Every person handles trauma and pain differently. We need to look with our hearts and not just our eyes. We must have compassion and understanding to be able to approach each person gently and personally. Heart hurt can last a lifetime if not healed and dealt with through the love of Jesus.

Our world was rocked that November day when Levi was born. Every person in our family was affected by Levi's health. I was struggling to be a happy parent and a broken one all at the same time, which was so hard on so many levels. I love all three of my boys immensely, and it was so hard to be there for all three at the same time. You physically can't be in three places at once, but God can; He is omnipresent. He can be there when we can't. His presence can encircle our loved ones and reach them when we can't. We must choose to pray, ask, and trust our heavenly Father to do this. He loves our children, our family, more than we even do. His desire for them and all of us is life, peace, joy, and fullness. He has plans to prosper us and not to harm us. He is the only true hope that exists. He is the Great I Am, the Prince of Peace. He is our comforter and healer and our hope.

My dear husband Ricky almost ran himself ragged trying to do everything during this time. His days of running and emotionally being there for all of us began to take their toll on his body, as he had a lot of people depending on Him. His employees, us, and Levi were all depending on him to show up. The weight that husbands and fathers carry is usually somewhat different from a mother. They carry the weight of protector and provider, feeling the pull to always be strong and not show weakness. Well, sometimes that is unrealistic and can be downright overwhelming.

Everyone needs time to weep and be human. We were created to have emotions and feelings, so it is not healthy to hold those in or to just let them spew out everywhere uncontrollably. We need balance, which helps us maintain a healthy mind and inner wellbeing by fully walking through what we feel when we feel it and not stuffing it down to deal with later. When we sit with Jesus and allow Him to minister to our spirits and minds in trials and pain, He can bring peace, peace that surpasses all understanding, to our souls and bodies when chaos is all around us. It is a supernatural thing that occurs and is a promise if we are His children.

The emotions we faced came in waves during Levi's hospital stay. It was like a tide pool. Sometimes we would be floating along enjoying the water, but then the waves would come and knock us clear out of the tube, under the water, and gasping for air. However, my heavenly Father would pick us right back up. For me, He held me, dried me off, or drifted with me for a while until I could regain my strength to get back on the float. He never, ever left me. Not one time. Sometimes I felt alone, but my faith and knowing the truth of His Word told me that He was there. This brought me comfort and endurance and gave me hope.

That evening after I left the hospital, on December 10th, they did another echo of Levi's heart. It showed it was beating too fast, and the beats were not strong beats. The cardiologist said his heart was not strong enough to endure the stress of eating and breathing together at the same time. His heart could not pump out the blood fast enough for the body to eat, breathe, and digest the food. So, the staff stopped all feeding and continued him on the blood pressure medicine. They did this to allow his heart to strengthen before they fed him again.

We met with the heart doctor, and they were puzzled with no answers or solutions. This was the common theme since Levi came into the world. No one could really explain anything. They really were unsure of what happened at birth or before birth to Levi and even in this moment ... the only thing I can come up with is that God allowed this to happen this way so that we would have to put our total trust and faith in Him because He is the ultimate healer. He had the answers, had Levi in the palm of His hand, and we had to trust Him completely.

*So shall my word be that goes out of my mouth; it shall not
return to me empty, but it shall accomplish that which I purpose, and shall succeed in the thing for which I sent it.
(Isaiah 55:11 ESV)*

I believed and held onto the word that God had promised to
completely heal Levi. We had already seen so many miracles. That
night, I sent out a plea on social media, a prayer. I wrote:

*Lord, right now I send out a prayer of complete healing over
his heart. I pray it beats strongly and properly. I pray that it
pumps efficiently and gets blood to every area it needs to. I
pray this medicine does good for his heart and does no harm.
We pray for a speedy recovery so he will be able to eat soon.
We send out this prayer and that it will not come back void
but that it will accomplish what it is set out to do, and that is
to heal Levi. Thank you for listening to our prayers. Amen.*

Because of my daily posts, a friend reached out to me and asked
about starting a prayer chain for Levi. She mentioned having everyone pray at a specific time. I loved this idea, and I knew God had
stirred her heart to ask this. I knew the power in praying together
and praying in unity. She sent out a text to her prayer chain, and I
put out a plea on social media asking everyone to share the post and
to pray at eight that night. We had several church prayer chains in-
volved as well as hundreds of friends praying with us. I asked them
to pray whatever way God led, but I also shared our specific needs
and desires for Levi's recovery. I asked them to pray for God's complete healing, for God to completely heal Levi's heart so that it
would work and pump perfectly, for his CRP to go down to normal,
for his lung function to be perfect, for complete healing from head
to toe, and that he would be home for Christmas.

We prayed big prayers and asked for big things because we believed in our big God, who could heal and make all things new. We

believed He was the same God who parted the Red Sea, who raised Jesus from the dead, and we believed He could heal Levi completely.

God had stirred our hearts, and He was stirring others. He orchestrated a shift. December 11th was the day the shift took place, the day we shook the heavens with our prayers. So that night at eight, all around the world, people were praying together, at the same time, in agreement, and crying out for the healing of our son!! This is when the major shift came. I believe this is when the full healing began and that this is when all of Heaven poured out on our Levi, and Jesus breathed His healing breath into Levi's body. This was a huge move toward His complete healing, as we began to see the shift and effects daily. This was the jumpstart that ignited the turnaround.

6

The Turnaround

THE TURNAROUND DID NOT HAPPEN ALL AT ONCE, BUT IT began to happen daily. You could feel a shift in the atmosphere. A shift in Levi's health. Daily, we would see a healing of one ailment or maybe two. Some days, we would get an answer. Some days, we would get none, but every day Levi began to get stronger, and we saw the Lord all over his life. Every breath was a gift. The prayers of others gave us strength, and I believe these prayers shifted Levi's recovery.

> *...pray for one another to be instantly healed, for tremendous power is released through the passionate, heartfelt prayer of a godly believer! (James 5:16, TPT)*

> *... pray for each other so that you may be healed. The earnest prayer of a righteous person has great power and produces wonderful results. (James 5:16, NLT)*

He began to be able to eat and function at the same time. Levi started to thrive and over the next twelve days, we saw more victories than defeats. We could physically feel the prayers, and we could feel the response from Heaven that they caused. On December 12th, the hospital staff did another echo of his heart. Levi's inflammation rate had jumped up again, even though they had moved the PICC line. They were hoping the echo would give them answers as to why his inflammation rate continued to rise.

That evening, he had a great night. When I came in that next morning, he was off the CPAP machine and was only on oxygen. I was ecstatic! They decided to try the feedings again. He had taken two bottles during the night, and I was able to nurse him twice that day!! This was a huge advancement. Just a couple days prior, he had not been able to eat, breathe, and digest the food, so this was another miracle. The cardiologist came in and gave us a good report. He was so impressed with how much Levi had improved in just two days.

By December 14th, when I walked into the NICU that morning, Levi had no tubes on his sweet face. He was free of all oxygen assistance, and the nurses were just beaming because he had had such a good night. His inflammation rate dropped from 22 to 17, and his blood pressure remained stable. They began to wean him with a lower dose of blood pressure medicine. They also began to increase his feedings. We continued to ask for prayers for his breathing to continue to strengthen and his body to be able to eat and breathe without struggling. God answered them all!!

I was blown away at the change we saw right before our eyes of Levi. I knew the prayers were working; the power of the presence of God was there. I saw His hand working. I physically felt God. We began to hear stories of how Levi's life and trials were touching many. People had been storming Heaven with their prayers and grown so dependent on God on behalf of Levi. People all around the globe were praying for him, crying out for our son ... for his life. One baby boy ... his life was touching so many. It was phenomenal to see God move, and I am humbled at the amount of people that rallied with us and for our boy. It was a miracle to see, and I am thankful that the Lord let me see how this trial touched so many. I could not thank people enough for praying. People would share his story on social media; small groups were gathered praying for him; churches and prayer chains all over had him on their list and lips!! The body of Christ is so strong when we pray together in unity. We bring down Heaven to earth when we declare His Word here. God's promises are good, but sometimes we must walk through the valley to see those promises in fruition. The path to the other side can be hard and literally, as I walked through the valley of the shadow of death, I had to remember His promises. He had promises for Levi's future, and I had to trust the Lord until we got there.

God's ways are much higher than ours. He works in mysterious ways; unbeknownst to man is the outcome of one's life. Our role as a Christian, a child of God, is to rely on, trust fully, surrender our will for His, forgive fully, love others, share the truth of the gospel, and fully and completely worship Him and bring Him honor and glory in all we do. Even when life is falling apart, we must trust Him and rely on Him. He is our source of life and strength. When we do this, even during turmoil, we will find Him. We will find peace and rest in His presence. He will never leave us.

Now I can look back and see some of what God was doing and orchestrating. I see His goodness in the pain and the blessing of His hand over us. I see what good came out of the trial. Great is Levi's reward for enduring so much to touch so many hearts for the Lord. When all was said and done, we could see why this path had to come to pass. We can see now how his precious life and journey impacted so many. God is good all the time.

Every day was new. Each day carried challenges of faith and blessings of favor. Every day, I was in awe of this child I got to call mine. This little warrior was thrown into a battle for his life at the exact moment of his birth. He was purchased with a price of blood by a spotless lamb, and his very birth shook the heart of our family and our community. People waited anxiously for the updates on our precious Levi. It is said it takes a village to raise a child; well, it did in this case as well. It took a village to raise him up from the very pit of death.

I would just sit and look at Levi in his NICU room and marvel at how such a tiny human could endure so much and still survive. The grace and goodness of God overwhelmed me in these moments of snuggling this little one. He looked so perfect on the outside, beautifully made with ten toes and ten little fingers. His sweet, little face. Oh, I think of Mary holding Jesus, as she beheld her son, so fragile yet still fully God. What she must have felt in those moments of nursing her son. Looking at his beautiful face and wondering about his fate. She carried much as being his mother. God hand-picked Mary. God had hand-picked me for Levi, as his birth carried a weight. Every birth of a child does, but when the very life that has been given is trying to be snuffed out, it's something different. It carries a heavy punch, changing the normalcy of birthing a child. It alters your reality and shifts your focus.

Everything that we take for granted comes crashing down. Just the simplicity of breathing that we take for granted becomes such an importance that you never even thought about being missed or taken. The life force of the breath of the Lord can hang in the balance of something we cannot control but only have faith and hope for. We can pray and continue to cling to our maker and in these moments, that is what you must choose to do. You must choose to cling to Him and His breath. We must lean back and lean against His chest and listen to His heartbeat and His breath to keep ours from stopping. He is the very source of life and peace; He is. We can search all over and never find it until we find Him. Not that He needs to be found because He comes after us, but there are times when we must lose all earthly things to see God clearly and see Him for who He really is.

Over the next few days, we began to see the miracles for Levi come rolling in. We began to see the daily impact of the prayers that everyone was praying. We saw the power of God, the evidence of His existence. We felt His breath of power blowing gently over Levi. The next half of his stay in the NICU was different from the first, as these days carried hope and promise. Levi continued to get better, and the hospital staff began to wean his dosage of the blood pressure medicine from a drip to an oral dose. This was a necessity to be able to go home. His pressure remained stable and good. The doctors said he had developed cardiomyopathy, which they believed had been caused by a virus in utero. They believed that the virus had attacked the heart and caused it to become weak, therefore causing his heart muscle to not be able to fully function properly. Without the blood pressure medicine, his heart could not function on its own. The medicine helped support the heart while it healed from the strain of the virus on his organs. His liver had also become enlarged.

Over a matter of days, we began to see God heal Levi's heart very quickly. God does not make mistakes, but sometimes terrible things happen in this life because we live in a world that is plagued by sickness and disease, because of man's sin. But God can, and will, use what the enemy means for harm, and for death, for the good of those who truly love and obey Him.

The results of Levi's echo showed that his heart was returning to normal size and beginning to heal. The doctors started the oral dose of meds, and his vitals remained stable. They also took him off all antibiotics and increased his feedings all in one day, and he did so well with the changes. Here was more evidence of his health turning around. The prayers, the power of God, were continually being released over us and Levi.

Sometimes our prayers can be the very song that we sing. It doesn't always have to be words spoken; sometimes it can be our very cry and tears we shed. The Lord sees our hearts and knows our desires. Yes, there is power when we speak our prayers and desires out loud, but sometimes when the words cannot come, when we do not know what to say, then the very Spirit of God that lives within us groans for us. There is power in submission. In our human mind and understanding, we feel weak in this way but in the heavenly realm, there is power in submission to God, especially in the laying down of our desires and wants and clinging to His will, His desires, and His ways.

When we are so in tune with Him and in a close relationship with Him, then our and His desires are meant to become as one. Just like in marriage, when a husband and wife become one, so do we, as we become one with God through Jesus Christ. He resides within our very being. His Spirit becomes one with ours through the sacrifice and power of the blood of Jesus Christ. When we submit to Him and join in unity with Him, we become one. We become yoked with

Him. There is an intimacy here that cannot completely be explained until fully experienced. This is a gift, a union, that cannot be broken by mere man or principalities of darkness. This is a spiritual bond, a blood pact, a commitment that is defined by scripture and by the very existence of Jesus's life.

> *And in a similar way, the Holy Spirit takes hold of us in our human frailty to empower us in our weakness. For example, at times we don't even know how to pray, or know the best things to ask for. But the Holy Spirit rises up within us to super-intercede on our behalf, pleading to God with emotional sighs too deep for words. (Romans 8:26, TPT)*

I truly believe God has given doctors wisdom in many things and ways, but I also know that our true source is God Himself. We must rely on Him completely and not put our trust or belief solely in doctors or modern medicine. We must fully rely on the Lord. With each moment and time in our lives, we must seek His face for the best option and course we should take, which can include earthly medicine and means. The doctors give you all the scenarios; the good, the bad and the ugly. Yet, God can heal however way He sees fit, so our trust needs not to be in man but in Him. I had to remember this many times.

The doctors came in that day telling me all the complications that "could" happen when switching from the drip medication to the oral dosage for Levi. All this information overwhelmed me. I overheard the doctor and nurses talking about what could happen and what to watch for … my heart became heavy with the news. I began to look at the circumstances, the what ifs, instead of the promises God had given us. I took my eyes off the good things that had already happened and put them on the bad things that could happen, I quickly became heavily burdened and engulfed in despair. I began to weep, so I closed the curtain of our little NICU area, and I nursed my baby. I placed him in his mamaRoo (love this thing) and began to pray to God. I felt defeated and felt as if my prayers were not going anywhere. I couldn't even think of the words to pray … So, I began to sing (softly). The words that came out of my mouth were straight from Heaven. This song, I believe, was gently given to me by the Holy Spirit for such a time as this one.

The very nature of God is good; His greatest attribute is love. His love for His children cannot fully be comprehended here on earth, but He gives us glimpses, promises, and moments of tender rawness where He comes in and covers us in love. This was one of those moments. The words flowed from my mouth in desperation and were covered in tears. With only a whisper, I could sing, and that is all it took for God to come close.

I just kept on singing and repeating these lyrics. Ever so gently and tenderly, God's presence filled that little space so thickly, it felt like a weighted blanket. I began to weep a different cry, a healing cry. It came from within as the Holy Spirit brought healing, peace, and rest to my heavy-laden soul. I was instantly soothed by His presence and His peace surrounding Levi and me. I looked at my sleeping baby and knew he was ok, and that, again, "God's got this". *Oh, how He loves us,* I thought … His tender mercies are new every morning, and they are intimate, timely, and always covered in love. The greatest of these is love.

Since Levi did so well with the switch, from drip to the oral dose, the doctors continued to increase his feedings. They wanted him to continue gaining strength and endurance and being able to eat was one of the best ways to accomplish that goal. I would nurse during the day while I was there with him, and then they would bottle-feed him at night. He continued to thrive and gain weight throughout the rest of his stay in the NICU. His inflammation rate continued to go down and improve as well. Levi was looking and thriving the way we had prayed so fervently for. We had prayed big prayers, specific moment-by-moment prayers, and we continued to see God answer those prayers. Not always the way we thought, but we knew He was always working for our good.

That evening as I left the hospital, I still cried. It never got any easier at night when I had to leave Levi … twenty-three days in the hospital, and I still cried the whole way to the car. I would have to force myself to leave; even the nurses would have to ask me to leave at 6:30 for shift change ... I would cry all the way home, as I left a piece of my heart behind in that little bed every night ... man, I can still feel that as I write these words now. It's different now, because I know the rest of the story, but it still carries a weight in my heart. Memories leave marks in our souls, and if they are not thoroughly touched and healed by the power of the Holy Spirit and the love of Jesus, then they can continue to cause pain. But with their heavenly touch, they can bring peace and hope. They can bring joy and a realization of the goodness of God.

The next day, they did an EKG, an echo, completely removed the drip of blood pressure medicine, and drew more blood to run tests. The EKG and the echo results looked good. The heart continued to heal and improve. His brain was showing good function without seizure activity. These results were breaths of fresh air to us. His troponin level rose in his bloodwork, which can indicate that there had been some damage to the heart.

The doctors decided to give Levi IVIG, which is intravenous immune globulin acquired through donors. Immunoglobulin is part of the blood's plasma and contains antibodies that help fight germs or disease. Having this infusion can help strengthen a weakened immune system. The doctors hoped the antibodies would help protect Levi's heart and keep the virus from causing more harm to the heart and his other organs. We prayed that his body would accept these infusions with no harmful side effects, and that the blood would only do good to Levi's little body. We also prayed it would help him thrive even more, and he did just that!! The next morning, I got a call from the cardiologist, who said Levi had, had a great night, and he had done well with everything, and his troponin level had already begun to come down! We saw him continue to heal.

As I went into the NICU that morning, the nurses informed me that they had a hard time getting Levi to sleep in his NICU bed at night ... he wanted to be held all the time. This was a result of me holding him all day. I mean, how could I put him down willingly?

It was a week before I even got to hold him for the first time after his birth and I was never with him at night, so what can I say? I never wanted to let go of him physically. I had already begun to spoil him. He still kind of is today ... but sometimes when things are hard and even scary, when things are almost lost or stolen, we hold these things more closely when they are returned or given back to us. We can truly see their worth and know the reality of life, that we are only here but for a vapor and then gone. Life is a gift and a treasure not to be taken for granted. Death and the fear of death can put things into perspective very quickly, aligning us where we have gotten out of alignment with what really matters in life.

Every day during this time, the doctors and nurses would walk by and marvel at our Levi. They could not believe how well he was doing. They would just come by his bed and look and smile. God was healing him right in front of their eyes. One doctor, who had left the country for a week, came by and said, "I cannot believe how good he looks. He was so sick when I left. I was afraid he would not even make it. Look at him now." Yes, look at him now! Look at what the Lord has done. We witnessed a miracle of God and saw firsthand His mighty work. Now that was a miracle and a blessing.

That night, as I lay in bed, I began to remember the prayers I had continually prayed for years for myself and our family. "Dear Lord, please make us a closer family. Lord, help me to be a better mother and wife. Lord, please draw Ricky and I closer to each other and closer to You. Please draw my boys closer to You and use them to do great things for You ... to reach hundreds, even thousands. Lord, soften my heart toward others, and help me see others the way You see them. Lord, use me to tell others about You and break my heart for what breaks Yours. Lord, refresh my soul and set my heart on fire for You. God, help me to trust You completely, and please take away my fears and anxieties..."

There are many more prayers that I have prayed, but these stand out to me the most in that moment. God reminded me of them, and I began to see that He had answered all these with the birth of a baby. Levi's life and trials had crashed and turned our world upside down but at the same time, it had brought healing and peace. God answered all these prayers in His time and in only a way that He could. I say it again, "Consider it pure joy my brothers when you face trials for the testing of your faith produces steadfastness." God has plans to prosper us and not to harm us. He has plans to give us a future and hope and no plans of evil toward His people.

Only two days later, I would need to remember that promise once again. I would need to remember all of them that we had heard throughout Levi's trial. We were about to face another blow, one that could bring death and defeat. God wasn't done yet.

7

Remembering the Promise

SO MANY TIMES, WE GET SO CAUGHT UP IN OUR DAILY lives, trials, or circumstances in which we are facing in the moment, or that season that we forget the promises of God. The promises He has spoken to us and over us. I walked in that morning so excited, so looking forward to hearing what the doctors had to say. Levi was doing so well. On December 21st, Levi had a repeat MRI and an MRV of his brain. We prayed that we would see a completely healed brain and prayed everything would look well.

We had to wait for the neurologist to read the report the following day, but the radiologist said it looked better than the first one. They believed that the stroke injury was healing. This was great news! He also had Levi's hearing test done, and he passed with flying colors. This was also incredible news. His troponin level increased again so we began to pray that it would come back down. All his other bloodwork was looking better, which was great! His inflammation rate was 1.2 and still needed to reduce a tad more, but it had continued to steadily drop, which was wonderful. We continued to pray for healing and strengthening of his heart. He was also doing well on the new medicine, and his blood pressure was staying normal and stable.

I went to sleep that night so full and happy. Levi was thriving, and all our prayers were being answered. I was ecstatic and relieved. The nurses told me to bring the car seat the next day … could it be that he would get to go home? Could December 22nd be the day we get to take our sweet Levi home? But hadn't the Lord told me that Levi would be home the night before Christmas? Maybe He was answering that promise a couple of days early. I hoped inside that was the case, but deep down in my spirit, I heard a still, small voice say, "It's not Christmas Eve yet. Remember My promise. He will be home the night before Christmas." But my flesh just pushed the thought aside. My flesh wanted to pick up my son and walk out of that hospital then. I didn't want to wait any longer for the healing. I wanted the completion now and wanted the promise right then to be fulfilled.

We have become so impatient in today's society, wanting everything now. We get so frustrated when things don't go our way and forget that God's plans are so much higher than ours. He takes His time and works all things out in His time. The next morning, December 22nd, I sat there waiting for the results of the MRI and MRV. I waited anxiously, excited with the expectation of finally taking our boy home. I heard the phone ring at the nurses' station behind me. We had been placed there, close to them, because of his needs. Levi had been so sick and facing death that we were placed directly across from them.

I heard the doctor take the phone and soon realized it was in response to Levi's results. I heard the doctor begin to respond. It sounded like his breath was being removed. I felt it; I felt the fear and sadness creep in. I felt the defeat come kicking and could tell he was receiving bad news. My heart began to shake. The doctor walked ever so slowly over like he had a load of cement blocks anchored to him. I could tell he carried a weight he didn't want to bear. He sat down beside me and told me the news. The tests revealed a blood clot in Levi's tiny brain; that will stop your heart. Those words can send a person into defeat and despair in an instant. The weight of those words brought a new kind of desperation and fear. How could this be his fate? Had he not suffered enough already? Did he really need to experience more pain? Did this child, who was not even a month old, need to face death yet again? This innocent child had faced more in the first month of his life than most people will ever face in their entire lives.

I wept and wept bitterly. I had no words; I could not pray but could only sit and cry. I felt like I had been hit again in the chest with a sledgehammer, the pain was overwhelming. Here we were so close to being able to go home. I sat there broken, yet once again. I sat there in that cold chair in front of Levi's little NICU bed and wept and wept. The nurses would walk by and cry as well for us. The doctor walked away, carrying his heavy load of news. The weight he must have felt. What kind of burden must it be to have to share that kind of news with a mother? Gosh, we never know what people are carrying at times.

I sat there, bewildered and shaken. I could not even muster a word, only tears. But in that moment, God, in all His goodness, provided an earthly angel. Her name was Hannah, which means favor and grace (babycenter.com). God showed me favor and grace by bringing Hannah, a family friend and a NICU nurse whose first day on first shift just happened to be this day, this day that we received such heart wrenching news. I have no doubt that God sent Hannah to us at just the right time and into our little area. She prayed over Levi and our situation, prayed the very heart of God over us. She was my voice when I could not speak. God provided; He had always provided. He always showed up, right on time. The Father continued to show me how much He loved me, even when the circumstances around us did not seem to reflect it.

The neurologist had seen a residual clot, which they think had caused the strokes, or it could have been caused by several different things: the trauma he endured, the head cooling, or the transfusions. They were hoping it would dissolve itself while he had been in the NICU, but it had not. The doctors had Levi transported to Greenville Hospital, which was one county over, to the children's wing for their specialty in hematology. They planned on giving him two shots a day of Lovenox, a blood thinner that would hopefully dissolve the clot.

I wish I could say that in this moment I was strong and that I had prayed the right prayer and said the right thing, but I did not. My soul was so overwhelmed, I questioned God. I was angry, hurt, and broken and could not understand why there was another set-back. We had seen so much progress, so much healing, and to be slapped by this news, it took my breath away. My husband came into the NICU and was strong. He said to me, "God has got this." I wanted to believe, I wanted to know, but I had again taken my eyes off the Creator and put it on the situation. There is no hope in the circumstances. There is no hope without the Lord. He is the way, the truth, and the life (John 14:6). He tells us to keep our eyes on Him, and He knows what we will do if we look away. Our flesh is weak and without His strength, there are times we will not survive. But thankfully He never leaves or forsakes us.

The transport team loaded our Levi into the box yet again; man, this felt like starting over. A strong reminder of where we started. A shot in the heart. My husband had brought our two other boys with him, expecting to bring our third son home that day. But instead of us leaving with him in a car seat, he left yet again in an ambulance and not with us. The transport team allowed our two older boys to see Levi before they left with him. They wheeled him out into the side hall and brought our boys around to see him, for the second time. Can you imagine from a child's standpoint what they must have felt? Did they fully understand what was even happening? Here lay their brother yet again, covered in wires and contained in a clear box on a stretcher with legs and wheels. And who knows what my face contained in that moment … the weight of it all was too heavy. I felt helpless to my sweet family that looked so broken. I felt obsolete.

I frantically drove to the next hospital, trying to arrive as soon as I could to be with Levi every step of the way. It was about a thirty-minute drive that felt like an eternity. I talked and cried out to God the entire way. I can honestly say I questioned God on this ride. I asked Him why. *Why did our sweet Levi have to face yet another battle for his life? Had he not suffered so much already?* My physical mind could not comprehend the reasoning why he was facing another feat with death. But God, in all His mercy, whispered, and I heard Him say to my spirit, "I am not done yet with Levi's story. We have one more miracle." I began to weep even harder, but this word, this rhema word, brought me hope. It reminded me of the promises already given. It reminded me that God was still in control and that I needed to pick Levi up and put him back into God's fully capable hands.

I asked God to hold me, our two other sweet boys, and my husband too. We needed rest and peace as well. We all needed healing within us. Our souls, my soul, needed a safe place from all the turmoil it felt and saw. God is our refuge and our strong tower. He is our resting place, and He will lay us beside still waters. Even though we may walk through the valley of the shadow of death, we will fear no evil for He is with us (Psalm 23). God will always provide for those who love Him, and He did. I just had to let go and let God do what He needed to do. I laid it all down, my worries, fears, hopes, and then I cried out and declared His promises!! I began to claim them over Levi and myself.

When we face many trials in life, we will not always respond to the way of joy at first, but we can alter our responses. We can't always change our circumstances, but we can choose the way we respond to them. When we choose to have faith or joy during what seems like defeat and death, it births something inside of us. It births hope, supernatural hope, and a pouring out from the heavens. The very God that created us and breathed life into us reaches down and scoops us up in His very capable hands. He gives us life and can give us peace and joy when all seems bleak.

We arrived at GHS. Here we were again in a new territory, frightening territory. BUT ... God was with us. Jesus rode all the way with Levi to the hospital, holding his hand, and now He had followed him all the way up to his room. Jesus had also ridden all the way with me. One of the wonderful things about God is that He is omnipresent, which means He can be everywhere at once. There is enough of Him to go around to everyone in need at any time!!

I was afraid, and that was ok. We can choose several ways to respond to fear. We can become frozen and not able to function; we can choose to run away from our circumstances; we can become so controlling that we begin to push everyone we love away; we can begin to mask our feelings with all kinds of substances or distractions; or we can let fear push us to the very feet of Jesus, where we lay down our circumstances and let Him work all things out for the good of those who love Him. Fear will always be there as we face uncertain things, but we can choose how we respond to it. We can become stronger and stronger in Him; this is what I chose to do here when facing such uncertainty. I chose to lay at Jesus's feet and let Him move. I rested knowing He was in charge. He could change things I could not. He could heal and protect me in ways I could not.

When you hear a diagnosis of a blood clot, it is scary. But when you hear about a twenty-nine-day-old infant with a blood clot in his brain, it is terrifying. The doctors always tell you the best outcome and the worst. We chose to claim the miracle. We chose to declare the healing. We were not giving up now, as we had come too far to let death weasel its way back in. This blood clot was just another battle we asked and trusted Jesus to win!

The first night at the next hospital was a blessing to me as well. It was the first time I got to spend the night with my son. I was able to be with him and not leave him at shift change. To think about what he must have felt during all of this, those thoughts can be overwhelming. A NICU can be a very scary place, with dim lights and buzzers going off constantly. New and strange faces peering down at you daily, sometimes minute by minute. You will hear those sounds for a long time even after you leave the NICU. A wave of defeat or even fear will hit you when you least expect it, as you wash your hands in a restroom with an automatic towel dispenser beside the same smell of antiseptic soap that reminds you of the washroom before entering the NICU. Our bodies can remember things in ways we don't expect. Sounds, smells, and our senses can set us off into a spiral of emotions if we do not properly identify them and bring them to the healing feet of Jesus. But here in this new hospital room, there were no buzzers, no other babies, just me and Levi. This was a gift, and I treasured every second I had with him, even if it was under uncertain circumstances.

That night, our family of five were finally all together. It was not the place I pictured or the way I wanted, but it was our reality. It was still good, still us together surrounded by what felt like chaos, but we were bound by love and family. We clung to each other and to the hope that we would soon be free of walls and wires. We cried, we laughed, and we were full even in the uncertainty.

That night, my husband took our other two boys home while I stayed the night with Levi. It was a rough first night together. Levi wanted to be held by me instead of laying in his hospital basinet, and my physical body needed rest. I hated to put him down and when I did, he cried. It was a typical mother-and-child scenario in that respect, but with an added list of overwhelming circumstances. Being in unknown surroundings made it more challenging and exhausting. But we were together, and for that, I was so thankful.

Over the next two days, I learned how to squeeze and maneuver the skin on my son's stomach in such a way to administer a shot of blood thinner into his abdomen. This was heart-wrenching to me. I had to sit and look at his sweet face as I caused him pain twice a day to try to save his life. He did not understand, and he would scream in pain every time I had to administer it. This again broke a part of me. We as parents want to save and protect our children and don't want to cause them pain, yet here I had to inflict pain to save his very life.

I believe this is a picture God had me see. Sometimes God steps back and allows times of pain and trials in our lives to allow us to be healed internally and for eternity. Does God want to cause us pain? NO! But because we live in a fallen world of sin and death, sometimes He allows the pain to bring about things that never could come to fruition any other way.

Levi's short life had been a whirlwind, with ups and downs, victories and battles, but we had learned so much in this short time. We had seen so much of God and had seen the power of God. We had witnessed the miracles of God, and now we waited for one more.

The Lovenox injections had to be administered twice a day, morning and evening. The levels in his system had to be just right to help dissolve the clot. If the dose was too strong, it could cause more issues and even death. If the dose was too small, then it could cause the clot to move, which could result in death, stroke, or even brain injury. The stakes were high, but we continued to trust God for the promises of Levi's full healing. We continued to pray and ask others to join us. Friends and families walked with us the whole way. If not in person, then they were online. They prayed, and they texted. They called, and they brought dinner. They were our support and community when our world was turned upside down. They helped us make it through this time. Community is a big deal. The enemy wants to isolate us from others and keep us bound, but God designed us to need each other. To need help and to need community. Ours was God sent.

That night in the hospital, I prayed for God's peace and presence to fill our room so thickly, and He did just that. We rested so much better because of His presence. God is so real and even though we are weak at times, He continues to be strong and unchanging. He is always good. We are never guaranteed tomorrow so we must live fully each day and love to the fullest.

December 24th, Christmas Eve morning: I had effectively administered two doses of medicine that day. The nurses assured me that I could continue to do this without their supervision at home. I was fearful but hopeful to be released. Until this point, every time they had checked his blood to see if the levels of medicine were acceptable, they had not been. They had been too high or too low. But at noon, the staff planned on doing another level check. If this level was considered normal, we could be free to go home. They also had scheduled another echo of his heart to ensure it was also continuing to heal and thrive. Gosh, we were praying and believing hard. Could we really go home? Could this be our Christmas miracle?

As I sat there waiting for the results of the echo and the blood-work, I began to remember the promise God had whispered to me so sweetly only a few weeks back. "He will be home the night before Christmas." Here it was, Christmas Eve, the night before Christmas. My heart leapt with joy and excitement. How had I forgotten so quickly this amazing promise? I had allowed our circumstances to flood my mind and heart and remove the seed the Lord had planted. *"When anyone hears the word of the kingdom and does not understand it the evil one comes and snatches away what was sown in his heart. This is what was sown along the path"* (Matthew 13:19 ESV).

That is what the enemy had done. He had come with his floods of lies and sickness. We had been bruised and battered, but we had built our house upon the rock, Jesus Christ. Our house may have been shaken, but it had not been torn down, for we had hope and mercy from Jesus Himself. And here we were, with what felt like an eternity of time that had passed, but here in a mere couple of weeks, God had completely transformed Levi in front of our eyes. We got to see a miracle; a present-day miracle took place within our hands. And guess what … the bloodwork was on point. And guess what … the echo looked great. And guess what … they let us take our precious Levi home on Christmas Eve!! The night, not the morning, but the night before Christmas, just like God had promised and whispered to my spirit. He never breaks His promises, never!! When God says something, it is so!!

We packed up our stuff and waited on the discharge papers. My husband brought in the car seat that had remained empty for one month. We placed our precious miracle, Levi Asher, into his car seat. We carried him out of the hospital with tears rolling down our faces and overwhelming joy in our hearts. We had been changed forever. We were so thankful and blessed. Our family was now complete. We finally were able to take our third son home with us. Now that was an incredible, unforgettable moment as we walked out of that hospital with all three of our sons. My heart was so full of emotions and gratitude.

God, in all His mercy and grace, had fulfilled His promise and helped us all along the way to hold on to it.

8

The Completion of the Miracle

OVER THE NEXT SIX WEEKS OF APPOINTMENTS, WE SAW God complete the miracle in Levi. We saw his heart return to normal size and look as if nothing had even taken place. We saw the blood clot vanish in six weeks and Levi was removed from every bit of medicine and did not require anything further. We saw the complete healing of Levi and saw him have no side effects from any medicine. We witnessed him having no long-term effects from lack of oxygen at birth and no physical or developmental delays. What we saw was a healthy baby completely perfect in every way. We watched him walk at nine months and got to see the miracle in all its fruition. Daily, we would stand in awe as we watched Levi grow and develop as if nothing had ever taken place. We got to see the power of Jesus's blood at work every day. We saw the healing, the power, the promises, the joy, the fullness of our Creator.

This trial, which ripped out our hearts at times, also brought about beauty I had never known before. It brought a glimpse of God daily into our homes. We saw the glory of God every day, and we still get to see it every day. Some days, I just sit in tears and watch Levi. I taste and see that the Lord is good. He is so good! He loves His children and wants to prosper them and not harm them.

Not every story turns out like Levi's, but God promises that He will always work things out for the good of those who love Him. He never ever leaves or forsakes us. He will uphold us by His mighty right hand. He commands His angels concerning you to guard you in all your ways. Jesus came so that we may have life and have it abundantly. Jesus defeated death, sickness, and disease on the cross. He died so we could live.

We also learned how to pray differently throughout this time. Jesus's disciples asked Him to teach them one thing while they were with Him for the three years that they walked together, and it was "Lord, teach us to pray…" (Luke 11:1). God taught us the power that we have in our very own mouths. We have the power to declare His promises and His living Word over ourselves.

> *…as it is written, "I have made you the father of many na-tions"—in the presence of the God in whom he [Abraham] be-lieved, who gives life to the dead and calls into existence the things that do not exist. In hope he believed that he should become the father of many nations, as he had been told, "So shall your offspring be." He did not weaken in faith when he considered his own body, which was as good as dead (since he was about a hundred years old), or when he considered the barrenness of Sarah's womb. No unbelief made him waver concerning the promise of God, but he grew strong in his faith as he gave glory to God, fully convinced that God was able to do what He had promised. That is why his faith was "counted to him as righteousness." But the words "it was counted to him" were not written for his sake alone, but for ours also. It will be counted to us who believe in Him who raised from the dead Jesus our Lord, who was delivered up for trespasses and raised for our justification." (Romans 4:17–25 ESV)*

We have the power of death and life in our very tongue. "The tongue can bring death or life," (Proverbs 18:21, NLT). There is so much power in a born again believer's words because of the author-ity Jesus has given us at the moment of our salvation. Many Chris-tians never even come close to walking in the power meant for us. We walk in fear, doubt, distractions, and sin. We were meant for so much more than just living day to day in comfortable living. We were meant to change the world through our words and our actions. We were designed for a purpose with a purpose, designed to bring Him glory. We were designed to share His good news with everyone we meet.

This trial of Levi's birth taught us the things that really mattered in life. God, our faith, our family, and how fragile and fleeting life really is. It removed all the distractions that had consumed our daily lives and exposed the purity, the very purpose of living. James 1:2 ESV says,

> Count it all joy, my brothers, when you meet trials of various kinds, for you know that the testing of your faith produces steadfastness. And let steadfastness have its full effect, that you may be perfect and complete, lacking in nothing.

It is hard to thank God for a trial during it, but there is power in doing that. It loosens you from the power of the circumstances and connects you to the power of your Savior instead. It brings joy and peace during a trial and pain.

This is when His love and mercies become so real. They cover you with such power that you feel them physically. This is when we begin to defeat the enemy. When we do the opposite of what our flesh wants to do, we loosen his grip on us and loosen the effects of his evil on our lives.

I know you may think this sounds good, but you may be thinking there is no way I can do this. I beseech you to try. I know firsthand the power in this. I chose both ways, and God saw me through both, but the power and the healing that came when I did as His Word led me to do was life changing. When we follow His Word, we can walk in the fullness of our salvation. The authority and power that He intended for us will be ours. Life will not always be easy. He gave us no promise of that for life, but there is a promise that no matter what we face, Jesus can give us peace. The kind of peace that fills you up and gives you hope during the most hopeless times.

Maybe you do not know this kind of peace that I speak of. Maybe you do not even know Jesus personally. You have heard about Him, possibly even prayed to Him, but you just feel an emptiness inside you. I want to invite you to change that right now. I want to invite you to have an intimate relationship with Jesus Christ. I want to help you find eternal peace and fullness in God through Jesus Christ. I encourage you to surrender your life, heart, and soul to Jesus. In the Bible, God's Word, it says, *"For God so loved the world, that he gave his only Son, that whoever believes in him should not perish but have eternal life" (John 3:16 ESV)*. It also says, *"If you confess with your mouth that Jesus is Lord and believe in your heart that God raised Him from the dead, you will be saved" (Romans 10:9 ESV)*. His Word also says, *"And now you must repent and turn back to God so that your sins will be removed, and so that times of refreshing will stream from the Lord's presence" (Acts 3:19, TPT)*. He promises to refresh us, cleanse us, forgive us, and save us from being separated from Him. We must open our mouths and speak. We must choose for ourselves life through Him.

If you desire this freedom, this peace, then I invite you to pray this very prayer out loud right now where you sit. You must truly mean it; don't let it just be lip service, but let it be a heartfelt prayer from the depths of your being. I want you to imagine Jesus is sitting in front of you right now, just like when I would picture Jesus standing beside Levi's bed. I would place Levi into the arms of Jesus every night so I could have peace to leave. I want you to find that same peace. I want you to know the Jesus I know. The one whose eyes are filled with love and hands carry gentleness and grace. His arms are strong, and His heart is full of compassion for you. Now, let's picture Jesus sitting across from you. Next, let's pray this prayer below out loud to Him.

Dear Lord,

I want to know you more. I desire to have true peace. I know I have messed up and sinned. I have struggled in this life to find purpose and fulfillment at times. My heart aches and desires for more. I am struggling to know the truth. I want to be friends with You, Jesus. I want to feel Your peace and love within my heart. Please forgive me of my sins, all of them. Lord, I repent of my sins, I want to be different. I want to follow You. I surrender my mind, my body, my soul, my spirit, and my heart to You. Jesus, I believe You died on the cross for me, so that I can be forgiven and be made righteous in the eyes of God. I believe Your blood is cleansing me right now as we speak, freeing and healing me from any sin, weight, heaviness, addiction, ailment, unworthiness, fear, doubt, guilt, rebellion, and anything that is not of You, God. I confess You as Lord and Savior of my life. I choose to walk in Your ways, read Your Word, sit and pray with You daily. I also choose to speak life over myself instead of death. I choose You, Jesus. I believe that Jesus died on the cross, rose again, and is now seated in Heaven with God. I ask that You fill me with Your Spirit. Holy Spirit, I ask that you baptize me and free me from any chain that has kept me bound and fill me with wisdom and truth.

Thank you for the gift of the Holy Spirit who has come as my helper. I ask for the gifts of the Spirit as I grow daily and walk in Your ways. I pray for courage and boldness as I share this good news with those around me and even through sharing this very prayer with others. I love you, Lord, with all that I am and all that is within me. Amen.

I am rejoicing right now!! Because for those of you who just prayed and surrendered your lives and hearts to Jesus. You have crossed over from death to life. You have walked from separation from God into daily communion with Him. Life is not guaranteed to be easier now, but He is promising to walk alongside you and never leave you. He will carry you, and He will comfort you when times are hard. He will bless you with peace and joy if you choose it. The promise of that is worth following Him daily. I could not have faced this trial with Levi without Him. He is the very air that I breathe. I am dependent on Him and am so thankful for Him and this trial.

Because of this trial, I can write this book. I can sit here with you and share this moment. I can share the very good news that He shared with me at the age of twelve. I am so thankful for you, and I am praying for each person who picks up this book. I pray that as you have read this book, you have felt the very presence of God in a fresh new way, maybe even for the very first time. I am praying that you encounter Him in supernatural ways. I pray that you get the miracle you are asking for in His mighty name.

The God who created me in His image and who loved me enough to save me when I was twelve, He never gave up on me, even as a young college kid who ran wild and away from Him. He is the God who never gave up on me when my marriage was falling apart. He is the same heavenly Father who never gave up on me when I was ready to give up during a deep depression. He is the supernatural Father who never left me or gave up on me when I lost all hope when our third son lay at death's doorstep! This God loves me! He has pursued me, hunted me down, and loved me uncondi-tionally, compassionately, and completely, no matter how I have be-haved! He loves me so much that He blessed me with the trial of Levi. He took what satan, the enemy, meant to destroy my son and me. He took it and prospered us. The pain, the suffering, the turmoil, the anguish, and the heartache. He can do the same for you and/or for someone you love!

God DOES allow us to face far more than we can handle. I could have ceased to exist at that moment, but I chose to cling to Him. I chose to cling to His promise that He will never leave us or forsake us. Would I have ever chosen this path? No. But He did for us, and He has drawn me so much closer to Himself and His peace than ever before. He had to break me to my core so He could heal me. I will never be the same, and I never want to be the same. I am so thankful that I have a baby to hold. I am so thankful for life itself. He has plans to prosper us into a closer relationship with Him and into His ever-lasting peace. He does not want to harm us. He wants to prepare us for spending eternity with Him. I am overwhelmed at His goodness. His gifts are not always wrapped in bows, sometimes they are not even wrapped at all. Sometimes they are thrown at you and leave you breathless and afraid, and we can't even tell that the pain is a gift because of how bad it hurts. But after the pain, and through the love and healing power of Jesus, comes peace, which is the greatest gift of all. Peace, the peace that only Jesus can give and nothing else compares.

Thank you for sharing your time with me and letting me share with you the story of Levi. This real-life story changed our world and hopefully has changed and impacted yours. I did not know if we would make it to this point, to this place of healing and resolution but we did. This trial radically altered our way of life and our spiritual reality of Jesus. This time of pain and turmoil that turned to healing and freedom could only be handwritten by God Himself. I pray, as you read *The Miracle of Levi*, you will see the goodness of God and His power as He transcends time and space to touch your heart through glimpses of His unconditional love and grace. I pray for miracles to break out in your life as you pursue Him intimately. May the God of the universe reach down from Heaven and touch you and your family in a very real way.

Levi is continuing to thrive and grow stronger every day. We still see the Lord's goodness in our daily lives. By retelling his story, I am reminded at how good God is and what a miracle Levi's story is. It is an honor for us to share what the Lord has done for us, and we are believing He can do the same for you or someone you love. May God bless you and your family.

HARP Initiative

BY WALKING THROUGH THIS PAIN AND TRAUMA IN MY life, not just the story of Levi, but life's bumps and bruises, I came across how good and powerful the love of Jesus really is. It radically changed my life and my perception of who God really is and what He can do. Through this journey of my life, God has brought healing and restoration to my soul, heart, mind, body, and spirit. I began to encounter the physical presence of the Lord which altered my personal relationship with Jesus Christ, God the Father, and my helper, the Holy Spirit. By placing my trust in Jesus and learning to listen to His voice, I have been able to help others walk through challenging times and overcome depression, anxiety, suicidal thoughts, lethargy, regret, sadness, complacency, lack of empathy, fear, defeat, and shame. By hearing the heart of the Father, through the still small voice in which He speaks, I can share His love for those that come for prayer. His love can heal parts of us that cannot be touched by the physical ways of this world.

My personal desire is to see people enter a personal relationship with Jesus Christ and for the entire body of Christ to walk in freedom and power through the Holy Spirit. I have tasted and seen that the Lord, Jesus Christ, is good, and I want to share that with everyone who will listen and believe. The intimacy that I have with Jesus is one that I want to help everyone cultivate. The healing that I have found through Jesus, from the trauma I faced and walked through, is one I want to help others experience as well.

Out of this healing and desperation, I had a dream to create a place of hope and healing. A place where I could share what God has done for me. A place where individuals can come and find rest. I had a dream to create a place where all things were good, lovely, and pure. This safe place is called HARP Initiative. It is a collection of good things. It is a family focused framework based on hope, truth, and love.

HARP Initiative also came from a place of desperation for more: more of God, peace, truth, Jesus, the Father's Heart, hearing His voice, His love, His tangible presence, and more of the power of the Holy Spirit. I wanted to create a place where truth is based upon the Word of God and not man's opinion. A place where people could come and find intimacy with Jesus. I dream of creating several books and resources that share my experiences and share the love and intimacy I have come to know with the Father, Jesus, and the Holy Spirit. One day I hope to have a refuge, a retreat center, where individuals can come and refresh, refuel, rest, and recharge. A place where Heaven meets earth. A sanctuary.

May God bless and keep you always in the palm of His hand. I pray that as you read *The Miracle of Levi,* that you will begin to see miracles from God. They are possible and at times they can happen right before our very own eyes. There is power when we surrender to His will and truly focus on His goodness and mercy. He has plans to prosper us and not to harm us. His nature is good even when the times and trials in our lives say otherwise, His relatability is ever present and attainable through His Son Jesus. His love is a gift. It is ours for the taking. God bless.

We would love to hear how Levi's story has impacted you. Please email us at harp.cassielittlejohn@gmail.com.

HARP Initiative LLC
www.harpinitiative.com

www.ingramcontent.com/pod-product-compliance
Lightning Source LLC
LaVergne TN
LVHW041324080426
835513LV00008B/588